THE YALE SHAKESPEARE

Revised Edition

General Editors

Helge Kökeritz and Charles T. Prouty

THE TRAGEDY OF
MACBETH

edited by Eugene M. Waith

LUX ET VERITAS

NEW HAVEN AND LONDON: YALE UNIVERSITY PRESS

Preface of the General Editors

AS the late Professor Tucker Brooke has observed, practically all modern editions of Shakespeare are 18th-century versions of the plays, based on the additions, alterations, and emendations of editors of that period. It has been our purpose, as it was Professor Brooke's, to give the modern reader Shakespeare's plays in the approximate form of their original appearance.

About half the plays appeared in quarto form before the publication of the First Folio in 1623. Thus for a large number of plays the only available text is that of the Folio. In the case of quarto plays our policy has been to use that text as the basis of the edition, unless it is clear that the text has been contaminated.

Interesting for us today is the fact that there are no act or scene divisions in the Quartos with the exception of *Othello*, which does mark Acts I, II, IV, and V but lacks indications of scenes. Even in the Folio, although act divisions are generally noted, only a part of the scenes are divided. In no case, either in Quarto or Folio, is there any indication of the place of action. The manifold scene divisions for the battle in such a play as *Antony and Cleopatra*, together with such locations as "Another part of the field," are the additions of the 18th century.

We have eliminated all indications of the place and time of action, because there is no authority for them in the originals and because Shakespeare gives such information, when it is requisite for understanding the play, through the dialogue of the actors. We have been sparing in our use of added scene and, in some cases, act divisions, because these frequently impede the flow of the action, which in Shakespeare's time was curiously like that of modern films.

Spelling has been modernized except when the original clearly indicates a pronunciation unlike our own, e.g. *desart* (desert), *divel* (devil), *banket* (banquet), and often in such Elizabethan syncopations as *stolne* (stol'n), and *tane* (ta'en). In reproducing such forms we have followed the inconsistent usage of the original.

We have also preserved the original capitalization when this is a part of the meaning. In like manner we have tended to adopt the lineation of the original in many cases where modern editors print prose as verse or verse as prose. We have, moreover, followed the original punctuation wherever it was practicable.

In verse we print a final *-ed* to indicate its full syllabic value, otherwise *'d*. In prose we have followed the inconsistencies of the original in this respect.

Our general practice has been to include in footnotes all information a reader needs for immediate understanding of the given page. In somewhat empiric fashion we repeat glosses as we think the reader needs to be reminded of the meaning. Further information is given in notes (indicated by the letter *N* in the footnotes) to be found at the back of each volume. Appendices deal with the text and sources of the play.

Square brackets indicate material not found in the original text. Long emendations or lines taken from another authoritative text of a play are indicated in the footnotes for the information of the reader. We have silently corrected obvious typographical errors.

vi

CONTENTS

[THE ACTORS' NAMES

DUNCAN, *King of Scotland*

MALCOLM
DONALBAIN } *his sons*

MACBETH
BANQUO } *generals of the king's army*

MACDUFF
LENNOX
ROSS
MENTETH } *noblemen of Scotland*
ANGUS
CATHNESS

FLEANCE, *son to Banquo*

SIWARD, *Earl of Northumberland, general of the English forces*

YOUNG SIWARD, *his son*

SEYTON, *an officer attending on Macbeth*

Boy, son to Macduff

An English Doctor

A Scotch Doctor

A Captain

A Porter

An Old Man

LADY MACBETH

LADY MACDUFF

Gentlewoman attending on Lady Macbeth

HECCAT

Three Witches

Lords, Gentlemen, Officers, Soldiers, Murtherers, Attendants, and Messengers; the Ghost of Banquo, and other Apparitions

SCENE: *Scotland; in IV.3, England*]

THE TRAGEDY OF MACBETH

Act I

SCENE 1

Thunder and lightning. Enter three Witches.

1 Witch. When shall we three meet again?
In thunder, lightning, or in rain?
2 Witch. When the hurlyburly's done,
When the battle's lost and won.
3 Witch. That will be ere the set of sun.   5
1 Witch. Where the place?
2 Witch.   Upon the heath.
3 Witch. There to meet with Macbeth.
1 Witch. I come, Graymalkin!
2 Witch. Paddock calls.
3 Witch. Anon!   10
All. Fair is foul, and foul is fair:
Hover through the fog and filthy air.   *Exeunt.*

SD **Thunder and lightning** N (SD is used throughout to indicate stage direction; N refers throughout to the corresponding note given at the end of the text.) 8–12 **Graymalkin . . . air** N. 10 **Anon** right away. SD **Alarum within** trumpet call off stage

SCENE 2

*Alarum within. Enter King [Duncan], Malcolm,
Donalbain, Lennox, with Attendants, meeting a
bleeding Captain.*

Duncan. What bloody man is that? He can report,
As seemeth by his plight, of the revolt
The newest state.
Malcolm.　　　　This is the sergeant,
Who like a good and hardy soldier fought
'Gainst my captivity. Hail, brave friend!　　　　5
Say to the king the knowledge of the broil
As thou didst leave it.
　Captain.　　　　Doubtful it stood,
As two spent swimmers, that do cling together
And choke their art. The merciless Macdonwald—
Worthy to be a rebel, for to that　　　　10
The multiplying villainies of nature
Do swarm upon him—from the Western Isles
Of kerns and gallowglasses is supplied;
And Fortune, on his damned quarrel smiling,
Show'd like a rebel's whore: but all's too weak;　　　　15
For brave Macbeth—well he deserves that name—
Disdaining Fortune, with his brandish'd steel,
Which smok'd with bloody execution,
Like Valor's minion carv'd out his passage
Till he fac'd the slave;　　　　20
Which nev'r shook hands, nor bade farewell to him,

3 sergeant three syllables N. 10 to that to make him so. 13 kerns
light-armored Irish foot soldiers. gallowglasses Irish armor-bear-
ers; F *Gallowgrosses.* 14 quarrel F *Quarry.* 18 execution five syllables. 19 minion (three syllables) favorite. 21 Which who N.

2

Till he unseam'd him from the nave to th' chops,
And fix'd his head upon our battlements.

Duncan. O valiant cousin! worthy gentleman!

Captain. As whence the sun 'gins his reflection 25
Shipwracking storms and direful thunders break,
So from that spring whence comfort seem'd to come
Discomfort swells. Mark, King of Scotland, mark:
No sooner Justice had, with valor arm'd, 29
Compell'd these skipping kerns to trust their heels,
But the Norweyan lord, surveying vantage,
With furbish'd arms and new supplies of men
Began a fresh assault.

Duncan. Dismay'd not this our captains, Macbeth
and Banquo?

Captain. Yes, as sparrows eagles, 35
Or the hare the lion.
If I say sooth, I must report they were
As cannons overcharg'd with double cracks,
So they doubly redoubled strokes upon the foe.
Except they meant to bathe in reeking wounds, 40
Or memorize another Golgotha,
I cannot tell—but I am faint,
My gashes cry for help.

Duncan. So well thy words become thee as thy
wounds; 44
They smack of honor both. Go, get him surgeons.

[*Exit Captain, attended.*]

---

22 **he** i.e. Macbeth. **unseam'd** ripped. **nave** navel. 25–6 **As whence
. . . thunders break** N. 25 **reflection** (four syllables) shining.
26 **break** F omits. 31 **surveying vantage** seeing his chance. 37 **sooth**
truth. 38 **cracks** explosions, i.e. charges. 40 **except** unless. **reeking**
steaming. 41 **memorize another Golgotha** N.

3

Enter Ross and Angus.

Who comes here?

   Malcolm.   The worthy Thane of Ross.

   Lennox. What a haste looks through his eyes!
So should he look that seems to speak things strange.

   Ross. God save the king!

   Duncan. Whence cam'st thou, worthy thane?

   Ross.   From
    Fife, great king;   50
Where the Norweyan banners flout the sky
And fan our people cold.
Norway himself, with terrible numbers,
Assisted by that most disloyal traitor,
The Thane of Cawdor, began a dismal conflict,   55
Till that Bellona's bridegroom, lapp'd in proof,
Confronted him with self-comparisons,
Point against point, rebellious arm 'gainst arm,
Curbing his lavish spirit; and to conclude,
The victory fell on us.

   Duncan.   Great happiness!   60

   Ross. That now Sweno, the Norways' king,
Craves composition;
Nor would we deign him burial of his men
Till he disbursed, at Saint Colme's Inch,

---

46 **Thane** N. 51–2 **flout . . . cold** N. 53 **Norway** the King of
Norway. 55 **dismal** disastrous. 56 **Bellona** goddess of war. **bride-**
groom i.e. Macbeth. **lapp'd in proof** clad in tested (proved)
armor. 57 **confronted him with self-comparisons** i.e. showed him
(Norway) his equal. 58 **rebellious** N. 59 **lavish** insolent. 61
Norways' Norwegians'. 62 **composition** (five syllables) a truce.
64 **Saint Colme's Inch** the island of Inchcolm in the Firth of
Forth.

4

Ten thousand dollars to our general use. 65

Duncan. No more that Thane of Cawdor shall deceive

Our bosom interest. Go pronounce his present death,
And with his former title greet Macbeth.

Ross. I'll see it done. 69

Duncan. What he hath lost noble Macbeth hath won. *Exeunt.*

SCENE 3

Thunder. Enter the three Witches.

1 Witch. Where hast thou been, sister?

2 Witch. Killing swine.

3 Witch. Sister, where thou?

1 Witch. A sailor's wife had chestnuts in her lap,
And munch'd, and munch'd, and munch'd: 'Give me,' quoth I: 5

'Aroint thee, witch!' the rump-fed ronyon cries.
Her husband's to Aleppo gone, master o' th' *Tiger:*
But in a sieve I'll thither sail,
And, like a rat without a tail,
I'll do, I'll do, and I'll do. 10

2 Witch. I'll give thee a wind.

1 Witch. Th' art kind.

3 Witch. And I another.

1 Witch. I myself have all the other;

---

65 **dollars** 16th-century German and Spanish currency (*thaler*). **general** read 'gen'ral' N. 66-7 **deceive . . . interest** N. 6 **Aroint thee** begone. **rump-fed** fat-rumped. **ronyon** term of abuse; literally 'scab.' 7 **Tiger** name of a ship. 14 **other** i.e. other winds.

And the very ports they blow,   15
All the quarters that they know
I' th' shipman's card.
I'll drain him dry as hay;
Sleep shall neither night nor day
Hang upon his penthouse lid;   20
He shall live a man forbid.
Weary sev'nights nine times nine
Shall he dwindle, peak and pine:
Though his bark cannot be lost,
Yet it shall be tempest-tost.   25
Look what I have.
  2 Witch. Show me, show me.
  1 Witch. Here I have a pilot's thumb,
Wrack'd as homeward he did come.   *Drum within.*
  3 Witch. A drum! a drum!   30
Macbeth doth come.
  All. The weyard sisters, hand in hand,
Posters of the sea and land,
Thus do go about, about,
Thrice to thine, and thrice to mine,   35
And thrice again, to make up nine.
Peace! the charm's wound up.

Enter Macbeth and Banquo.

  Macbeth. So foul and fair a day I have not seen.
  Banquo. How far is't call'd to Forres? What are
    these,
So wither'd and so wild in their attire,   40

15 **ports they blow** ports to which they blow (?) N. 17 **card** dial of
the compass. 20 **penthouse lid** eyelid N. 21 **forbid** accursed.
23 **peak** waste away. 32 **weyard** weird; F *weyward* N. 33 **Posters**
persons who ride posthaste. 35–6 **thrice to thine . . . to make up
nine** N. 39 **Forres** F *Soris.*

That look not like th' inhabitants o' th' earth,
And yet are on't? Live you? or are you aught
That man may question? You seem to understand
   me,
By each at once her choppy finger laying
Upon her skinny lips. You should be women,   45
And yet your beards forbid me to interpret
That you are so.
   Macbeth.   Speak, if you can: what are you?
   1 Witch. All hail, Macbeth! hail to thee, Thane of
      Glamis!
   2 Witch. All hail, Macbeth! hail to thee, Thane of
      Cawdor!
   3 Witch. All hail, Macbeth, that shalt be king here-
      after!   50
   Banquo. Good sir, why do you start, and seem to
      fear
Things that do sound so fair? I' th' name of truth,
Are ye fantastical, or that indeed
Which outwardly ye show? My noble partner   54
You greet with present grace and great prediction
Of noble having and of royal hope,
That he seems rapt withal; to me you speak not.
If you can look into the seeds of time,
And say which grain will grow and which will not,
Speak then to me, who neither beg nor fear   60
Your favors nor your hate.
   1 Witch. Hail!
   2 Witch. Hail!
   3 Witch. Hail!
   1 Witch. Lesser than Macbeth, and greater.   65
   2 Witch. Not so happy, yet much happier.

44 **choppy** chapped, cracked. 46 **beards** N. 53 **fantastical** imaginary. 56 **having** estate. 57 **rapt withal** transported by it.

3 Witch. Thou shalt get kings, though thou be
none.

So, all hail, Macbeth and Banquo!

1 Witch. Banquo and Macbeth, all hail!

Macbeth. Stay, you imperfect speakers, tell me
more.   70

By Sinel's death I know I am Thane of Glamis;
But how of Cawdor? the Thane of Cawdor lives,
A prosperous gentleman; and to be king
Stands not within the prospect of belief
No more than to be Cawdor. Say from whence   75
You owe this strange intelligence, or why
Upon this blasted heath you stop our way
With such prophetic greeting. Speak, I charge you.

Witches vanish.

Banquo. The earth hath bubbles, as the water has,
And these are of them. Whither are they vanish'd?

Macbeth. Into the air, and what seem'd corporal
Melted, as breath into the wind.
Would they had stay'd!

Banquo. Were such things here as we do speak
about?

Or have we eaten on the insane root   85
That takes the reason prisoner?

Macbeth. Your children shall be kings.

Banquo.   You shall be
king.

Macbeth. And Thane of Cawdor too; went it not
so?

Banquo. To th' selfsame tune and words. Who's
here?   89

67 get beget. 71 Sinel Macbeth's father. 81 corporal corporeal.
85 insane causing insanity as, e.g., hemlock was supposed to do.

Enter Ross and Angus.

Ross. The king hath happily receiv'd, Macbeth,
The news of thy success; and when he reads
Thy personal venture in the rebels' fight,
His wonders and his praises do contend
Which should be thine, or his. Silenc'd with that,
In viewing o'er the rest o' th' selfsame day,　　　95
He finds thee in the stout Norweyan ranks,
Nothing afeard of what thyself didst make,
Strange images of death. As thick as hail
Came post with post, and every one did bear
Thy praises in his kingdom's great defense,　　　100
And pour'd them down before him.

Angus.　　　　　　　　　We are sent
To give thee from our royal master thanks;
Only to herald thee into his sight,
Not pay thee.

Ross. And, for an earnest of a greater honor,　　105
He bade me, from him, call thee Thane of Cawdor;
In which addition, hail, most worthy thane!
For it is thine.

Banquo.　　　What, can the devil speak true?

Macbeth. The Thane of Cawdor lives;
Why do you dress me in borrowed robes?　　　110

Angus. Who was the thane lives yet;
But under heavy judgment bears that life
Which he deserves to lose.

93–4 His wonders . . . Silenc'd with that N. 98 images of death
i.e. those killed by Macbeth; F punctuates *death, as.* 98–9 hail/
Came F *Tale/Can.* 105 earnest pledge. 107 addition title. 108
devil (one syllable here) often spelled and pronounced 'divel.'

Whether he was combin'd with those of Norway,   115
Or did line the rebel with hidden help
And vantage, or that with both he labor'd
In his country's wrack, I know not;
But treasons capital, confess'd and prov'd,
Have overthrown him.

  Macbeth. [*Aside.*]   Glamis, and Thane of Cawdor:
The greatest is behind.

        [*To Ross and Angus.*] Thanks for your pains.
[*To Banquo.*] Do you not hope your children shall
    be kings,   121
When those that gave the Thane of Cawdor to me
Promis'd no less to them?

  Banquo.   That, trusted home,
Might yet enkindle you unto the crown,
Besides the Thane of Cawdor. But 'tis strange: 125
And oftentimes, to win us to our harm,
The instruments of darkness tell us truths,
Win us with honest trifles, to betray's
In deepest consequence.   129
Cousins, a word, I pray you.

  Macbeth. [*Aside.*]   Two truths are told,
As happy prologues to the swelling act
Of the imperial theme.—I thank you, gentlemen.—
[*Aside.*] This supernatural soliciting
Cannot be ill, cannot be good; if ill,
Why hath it given me earnest of success,   135
Commencing in a truth? I am Thane of Cawdor.
If good, why do I yield to that suggestion
Whose horrid image doth unfix my hair

115 line reinforce. 117 wrack ruin. 123 home to the utmost.
129 In deepest consequence in matters of the gravest importance.
131 swelling stately; see *Henry V*, Prologue, 3–4. 133 soliciting
prompting.

And make my seated heart knock at my ribs,
Against the use of nature? Present fears   140
Are less than horrible imaginings:
My thought, whose murther yet is but fantastical,
Shakes so my single state of man
That function is smother'd in surmise,
And nothing is but what is not.   145
   Banquo. Look how our partner's rapt.
   Macbeth. [*Aside.*] If chance will have me king, why,
     chance may crown me,
Without my stir.
   Banquo.   New honors come upon him,
Like our strange garments, cleave not to their mold
But with the aid of use.
   Macbeth. [*Aside.*]   Come what come may,   150
Time and the hour runs through the roughest day.
   Banquo. Worthy Macbeth, we stay upon your
     leisure.
   Macbeth. Give me your favor;
My dull brain was wrought with things forgotten.
Kind gentlemen, your pains are register'd   155
Where every day I turn the leaf to read them.
Let us toward the king.
[*To Banquo.*] Think upon what hath chanc'd; and,
     at more time,
The interim having weigh'd it, let us speak
Our free hearts each to other.

139 **seated** firmly fixed. 140 **Against . . . nature** contrary to natural habit. 142 **murther** common Elizabethan variant of 'murder.' **fantastical** imaginary. 143–6 **Shakes . . . rapt** N. 143 **single state of man** N. **single**, undivided, unbroken. 144 **function** normal activity of mind and body. 149 **strange** unfamiliar, new. **their mold** i.e. the body. 150–1 **Come . . . day** N. 150 **runs** alternative plural form. 153 **favor** pardon. 154 **wrought** troubled.

Banquo.   Very gladly.   160
Macbeth. Till then, enough. Come, friends. *Exeunt.*

SCENE 4

*Flourish. Enter King, Lennox, Malcolm, Donalbain,
and Attendants.*

Duncan. Is execution done on Cawdor?
Are not those in commission yet return'd?
 Malcolm. My liege, they are not yet come back.
But I have spoke with one that saw him die;
Who did report that very frankly he   5
Confess'd his treasons, implor'd your highness' par-
 don,
And set forth a deep repentance.
Nothing in his life became him
Like the leaving it. He died
As one that had been studied in his death   10
To throw away the dearest thing he ow'd
As 'twere a careless trifle.
 Duncan.   There's no art
To find the mind's construction in the face:
He was a gentleman on whom I built
An absolute trust.

            Enter Macbeth, Banquo, Ross, and Angus.
                         O worthiest cousin,   15
The sin of my ingratitude even now
Was heavy on me. Thou art so far before,
That swiftest wing of recompense is slow

SD Flourish trumpet fanfare. 2 Are F *Or.* in commission charged
with the duty. 10 had been studied had trained himself. 11 ow'd
owned. 17 before ahead.
    12

To overtake thee. Would thou hadst less deserv'd,
That the proportion both of thanks and payment
Might have been mine! only I have left to say, 21
More is thy due than more than all can pay.

Macbeth. The service and the loyalty I owe,
In doing it, pays itself.
Your highness' part is to receive our duties; 25
And our duties are to your throne and state,
Children and servants, which do but what they
          should,
By doing everything safe toward your love
And honor.

Duncan.   Welcome hither:
I have begun to plant thee, and will labor 30
To make thee full of growing. Noble Banquo,
That hast no less deserv'd, nor must be known
No less to have done so, let me infold thee
And hold thee to my heart.

Banquo.   There if I grow,
The harvest is your own.

Duncan.   My plenteous joys, 35
Wanton in fullness, seek to hide themselves
In drops of sorrow. Sons, kinsmen, thanes,
And you whose places are the nearest, know
We will establish our estate upon
Our eldest, Malcolm, whom we name hereafter 40
The Prince of Cumberland; which honor must
Not unaccompanied invest him only,
But signs of nobleness, like stars, shall shine
On all deservers. From hence to Inverness,
And bind us further to you. 45

20–1 That . . . mine N. 21 I have read 'I've' N. 28 **safe toward**
to guarantee. 36 **Wanton** unrestrained. 39 **establish our estate**
settle the succession. 41 **Prince of Cumberland** N.

Macbeth. The rest is labor, which is not us'd for
you:
I'll be myself the harbinger, and make joyful
The hearing of my wife with your approach;
So, humbly take my leave.
Duncan. My worthy Cawdor!
Macbeth. [*Aside.*] The Prince of Cumberland! that
is a step　　　　　　　　　　　　　　　　　50
On which I must fall down, or else o'er-leap;
For in my way it lies. Stars, hide your fires;
Let not light see my black and deep desires;
The eye wink at the hand; yet let that be　　　54
Which the eye fears, when it is done, to see. *Exit.*
Duncan. True, worthy Banquo; he is full so valiant,
And in his commendations I am fed:
It is a banquet to me. Let's after him,
Whose care is gone before to bid us welcome:
It is a peerless kinsman. *Flourish. Exeunt.*

SCENE 5

Enter Macbeth's Wife alone, with a letter.

Lady Macbeth. 'They met me in the day of success;
and I have learn'd by the perfect'st report, they
have more in them than mortal knowledge. When I
burn'd in desire to question them further, they made
themselves air, into which they vanish'd. Whiles I
stood rapt in the wonder of it, came missives from
the king, who all-hail'd me, "Thane of Cawdor," by
which title, before, these weyard sisters saluted me,

46 The rest . . . for you N. rest repose. 48 your approach i.e.
news of your approach. 6 missives messengers. 8 weyard F
weyward.

14

and referred me to the coming on of time with "Hail,
king that shalt be!" This have I thought good to
deliver thee, my dearest partner of greatness, that
thou mightst not lose the dues of rejoicing by being
ignorant of what greatness is promis'd thee. Lay it
to thy heart, and farewell.'

Glamis thou art, and Cawdor, and shalt be   15
What thou art promis'd. Yet do I fear thy nature;
It is too full o' th' milk of human kindness
To catch the nearest way. Thou wouldst be great,
Art not without ambition, but without
The illness should attend it. What thou wouldst
        highly   20
That wouldst thou holily; wouldst not play false,
And yet wouldst wrongly win.
Thou'dst have, great Glamis, that which cries,
'Thus thou must do,' if thou have it,
And that which rather thou dost fear to do   25
Than wishest should be undone. Hie thee hither,
That I may pour my spirits in thine ear,
And chastise with the valor of my tongue
All that impedes thee from the golden round,
Which Fate and metaphysical aid doth seem   30
To have thee crown'd withal.

Enter Messenger.

                         What is your tidings?
Messenger. The king comes here tonight.
Lady Macbeth.   Thou'rt
        mad to say it.

11 **deliver** report to. 15 **shalt** wilt. 18 **catch the nearest way** take
the shortest route. 20 **The illness should** the wickedness which
should. 23–6 **Thou'dst have . . . undone** N. 28 **chastise**
stressed ´ —. 29 **round** i.e. crown. 30 **metaphysical** supernatural.

Is not thy master with him? who, were't so,
Would have inform'd for preparation.

  Messenger. So please you, it is true; our thane is
    coming;   **35**
One of my fellows had the speed of him,
Who, almost dead for breath, had scarcely more
Than would make up his message.

  Lady Macbeth.   Give him tending;
He brings great news.   *Exit Messenger.*
              The raven himself is hoarse
That croaks the fatal entrance of Duncan   **40**
Under my battlements. Come, you spirits
That tend on mortal thoughts, unsex me here,
And fill me from the crown to the toe top-full
Of direst cruelty! Make thick my blood,
Stop up th' access and passage to remorse,   **45**
That no compunctious visitings of nature
Shake my fell purpose, nor keep peace between
Th' effect and it! Come to my woman's breasts,
And take my milk for gall, you murth'ring ministers,
Wherever in your sightless substances   **50**
You wait on nature's mischief! Come, thick Night,
And pall thee in the dunnest smoke of hell,
That my keen knife see not the wound it makes,
Nor Heaven peep through the blanket of the dark,
To cry 'Hold, hold!'

               Enter Macbeth.

        Great Glamis! worthy Cawdor!   **55**

34 **preparation** five syllables. 36 **had the speed of** outspeeded.
39 **raven** N. 40 **entrance** perhaps three syllables here. 42 **mortal**
murderous. 47–8 **keep . . . it** N. 48 **it** F *hit.* 49 **take** exchange.
50 **sightless** invisible. 52 **pall** enshroud. **dunnest** murkiest.

  16

Greater than both, by the all-hail hereafter!
Thy letters have transported me beyond
This ignorant present, and I feel now
The future in the instant.

 Macbeth.   My dearest love, **59**
Duncan comes here tonight.

 Lady Macbeth.   And when goes hence?

 Macbeth. Tomorrow, as he purposes.

 Lady Macbeth.   O, never
Shall sun that morrow see!
Your face, my thane, is as a book where men
May read strange matters. To beguile the time,
Look like the time; bear welcome in your eye, **63**
Your hand, your tongue: look like th' innocent
   flower,
But be the serpent under't. He that's coming
Must be provided for; and you shall put
This night's great business into my dispatch;
Which shall to all our nights and days to come **70**
Give solely sovereign sway and masterdom.

 Macbeth. We will speak further.

 Lady Macbeth.   Only look up clear;
To alter favor ever is to fear.
Leave all the rest to me.   *Exeunt.*

---

56 hereafter following, i.e. the third *all-hail*. **64 To beguile the time** F punctuates *matters, to beguile the time* N. **69 dispatch** management. **72 clear** with unclouded face. **73 favor** facial expression.

SCENE 6

Hoboyes and torches. Enter King, Malcolm, Donalbain, Banquo, Lennox, Macduff, Ross, Angus, and Attendants.

Duncan. This castle hath a pleasant seat; the air
Nimbly and sweetly recommends itself
Unto our gentle senses.
    Banquo.   This guest of summer,
The temple-haunting martlet, does approve
By his lov'd mansionry that the heavens' breath   5
Smells wooingly here; no jutty, frieze,
Buttress, nor coign of vantage, but this bird
Hath made his pendent bed and procreant cradle:
Where they most breed and haunt, I have observ'd
The air is delicate.

Enter Lady.

    Duncan.   See, see, our honor'd hostess!   10
The love that follows us sometime is our trouble,
Which still we thank as love. Herein I teach you
How you shall bid God eyld us for your pains,
And thank us for your trouble.
    Lady Macbeth.   All our service,
In every point twice done, and then done double,   15
Were poor and single business, to contend

SD **Hoboyes** (phonetic spelling of 'hautboys') woodwind instruments, related to modern oboe. **torches** N. 1 **seat** situation. 4 **martlet** F *Barlet* N. **approve** prove. 5 **mansionry** home-building. 6 **jutty** projection. 7 **coign of vantage** advantageous projecting corner. 8 **procreant cradle** cradle where he breeds. 9 **most** F *must*. 11–14 **The love . . . trouble** N. 13 **eyld** (probably pronounced 'eeld') reward. 16 **single** trivial.

Against those honors deep and broad
Wherewith your majesty loads our house.
For those of old, and the late dignities
Heap'd up to them, we rest your ermites.   20
   Duncan. Where's the Thane of Cawdor?
We cours'd him at the heels, and had a purpose
To be his purveyor; but he rides well,
And his great love, sharp as his spur, hath holp him
To his home before us. Fair and noble hostess,   25
We are your guest tonight.
   Lady Macbeth.   Your servants ever
Have theirs, themselves, and what is theirs, in compt,
To make their audit at your highness' pleasure,
Still to return your own.
   Duncan.   Give me your hand;
Conduct me to mine host: we love him highly,   30
And shall continue our graces towards him.
By your leave, hostess.   *Exeunt.*

SCENE 7

*Hoboyes. Torches. Enter a Sewer, and divers
Servants with dishes and service over the stage.
Then enter Macbeth.*

   Macbeth. If it were done, when 'tis done, then
    'twere well
It were done quickly. If th' assassination

---

20 **ermites** hermits, i.e. to pray for you. 22 **cours'd** rode after.
23 **purveyor** stressed $\acute{-}-\acute{-}$ N. 24 **holp** helped. 27 **Have . . . in
compt** (pronounced 'count') hold . . . accountable. **theirs** their
retainers. 29 **still** always. 31 **our** probably disyllabic here. SD
Sewer chief butler.

Could trammel up the consequence, and catch
With his surcease success: that but this blow
Might be the be-all and the end-all——here,   5
But here, upon this bank and shoal of time,
We'd jump the life to come. But in these cases
We still have judgment here; that we but teach
Bloody instructions, which being taught, return
To plague th' inventor. This even-handed justice   10
Commends th' ingredients of our poison'd chalice
To our own lips. He's here in double trust:
First, as I am his kinsman and his subject,
Strong both against the deed; then, as his host,   14
Who should against his murtherer shut the door,
Not bear the knife myself. Besides, this Duncan
Hath borne his faculties so meek, hath been
So clear in his great office, that his virtues
Will plead like angels, trumpet-tongu'd against
The deep damnation of his taking-off;   20
And Pity, like a naked new-born babe,
Striding the blast, or heaven's cherubin, hors'd
Upon the sightless couriers of the air,
Shall blow the horrid deed in every eye,
That tears shall drown the wind. I have no spur   25
To prick the sides of my intent, but only
Vaulting ambition, which o'er-leaps itself
And falls on th' other.

Enter Lady.

---

3 **trammel up** hold, as in a net; hamper. 4 **his surcease** N. 5–7
here . . . come N. 6 **shoal** F *Schoole* (a 17th-century spelling of
shoal). 7 **jump** risk. 8 **have judgment** receive sentence N. 17
faculties powers. 18 **clear** blameless. 22–3 **heaven's . . . air** N.
23 **sightless** invisible. 27–8 **Vaulting ambition . . . on th' other** N.

How now? What news?

Lady Macbeth. He has almost supp'd. Why have
you left the chamber?

Macbeth. Hath he ask'd for me?

Lady Macbeth.   Know you not he
has?   30

Macbeth. We will proceed no further in this business;

He hath honor'd me of late, and I have bought
Golden opinions from all sorts of people,
Which would be worn now in their newest gloss,
Not cast aside so soon.

Lady Macbeth.   Was the hope drunk   35
Wherein you dress'd yourself? Hath it slept since?
And wakes it now to look so green and pale
At what it did so freely? From this time
Such I account thy love. Art thou afeard
To be the same in thine own act and valor   40
As thou art in desire? Wouldst thou have that
Which thou esteem'st the ornament of life,
And live a coward in thine own esteem,
Letting 'I dare not' wait upon 'I would,'
Like the poor cat i' th' adage?

Macbeth.   Prithee, peace.   45
I dare do all that may become a man;
Who dares do more is none.

Lady Macbeth.   What beast was't then
That made you break this enterprise to me?
When you durst do it then you were a man;
And, to be more than what you were, you would   50
Be so much more the man. Nor time nor place
Did then adhere, and yet you would make both:

45 cat i' th' adage N. 47 do F *no* N. 48 **break** broach. 52 **adhere**
suit.

                                                        21

They have made themselves, and that their fitness
  now
Does unmake you. I have given suck, and know   54
How tender 'tis to love the babe that milks me—
I would, while it was smiling in my face,
Have pluck'd my nipple from his boneless gums,
And dash'd the brains out, had I so sworn
As you have done to this.
  Macbeth.   If we should fail?
  Lady Macbeth.   We fail?
But screw your courage to the sticking-place,   60
And we'll not fail. When Duncan is asleep—
Whereto the rather shall his day's hard journey
Soundly invite him—his two chamberlains
Will I with wine and wassail so convince
That memory, the warder of the brain,   65
Shall be a fume, and the receipt of reason
A limbeck only. When in swinish sleep
Their drenched natures lies as in a death,
What cannot you and I perform upon
Th' unguarded Duncan? what not put upon   70
His spongy officers, who shall bear the guilt
Of our great quell?
  Macbeth.   Bring forth men-children only;
For thy undaunted mettle should compose
Nothing but males. Will it not be receiv'd   74
When we have mark'd with blood those sleepy two
Of his own chamber, and us'd their very daggers,

53 that their fitness that fitness of time and place. 54 unmake un-
nerve. 60 But only. sticking-place N. 64 convince overpower.
65–7 memory . . . only N. 66 receipt receptacle. 67 limbeck
alembic, an apparatus formerly used in distilling. 68 lies lie. 71
spongy drunken. 72 quell killing. 73 mettle (same word as 'metal')
substance, spirit. 74 males pun on 'mails,' the metal rings of
which mail armor was composed. receiv'd understood.

That they have done't?

    Lady Macbeth.   Who dares receive it other,
As we shall make our griefs and clamor roar
Upon his death?

    Macbeth.   I am settled, and bend up
Each corporal agent to this terrible feat.   80
Away, and mock the time with fairest show:
False face must hide what the false heart doth know.

                                Exeunt.

77 other otherwise. **80 corporal agent** bodily faculty. **81 time**
world; see I.5.64–5.

Act II

SCENE 1

Enter Banquo, and Fleance with a torch before him.

Banquo. How goes the night, boy?
Fleance. The moon is down; I have not heard the
    clock.
Banquo. And she goes down at twelve.
Fleance. I take't, 'tis later, sir.
Banquo.   Hold, take my
    sword.
There's husbandry in heaven;   5
Their candles are all out. Take thee that too.
A heavy summons lies like lead upon me,
And yet I would not sleep.
Merciful powers, restrain in me the cursed thoughts
That nature gives way to in repose.   10

Enter Macbeth, and a Servant with a torch.

Give me my sword. Who's there?
Macbeth.   A friend.
Banquo. What, sir, not yet at rest? The king's
    a-bed.
He hath been in unusual pleasure,
And sent forth great largess to your offices.

SD **torch** i.e. torchbearer. 5 **husbandry** economy. 6 **that** i.e. **a**
shield (?) or cloak (?). 7 **summons** i.e. to sleep. 14 **largess** gifts.
offices servants' quarters.
    24

This diamond he greets your wife withal,   15
By the name of most kind hostess, and shut up
In measureless content.
    Macbeth.   Being unprepar'd,
Our will became the servant to defect,
Which else should free have wrought.
    Banquo.   All's well.
I dreamt last night of the three weyard sisters: 20
To you they have show'd some truth.
    Macbeth.   I think not of
    them.
Yet, when we can entreat an hour to serve,
We would spend it in some words upon that business,
If you would grant the time.
    Banquo.   At your kind'st leisure.
    Macbeth. If you shall cleave to my consent, when
    'tis,   25
It shall make honor for you.
    Banquo.   So I lose none
In seeking to augment it, but still keep
My bosom franchis'd and allegiance clear,
I shall be counsell'd.
    Macbeth.   Good repose the while!
    Banquo. Thanks, sir: the like to you.   30
                  Exit Banquo [with Fleance.]
    Macbeth. Go bid thy mistress, when my drink is
    ready
She strike upon the bell. Get thee to bed.
                      Exit [Servant.]
Is this a dagger which I see before me,

16 shut up ended (his remarks or his day). **17–19 Being . . .
wrought** N. **20 weyard** F *weyward*. **25 cleave . . . 'tis** be of my
party when the time comes. **28 franchis'd** free of blame.

The handle toward my hand? Come, let me clutch
    thee.
I have thee not, and yet I see thee still.   35
Art thou not, fatal vision, sensible
To feeling as to sight? or art thou but
A dagger of the mind, a false creation,
Proceeding from the heat-oppressed brain?
I see thee yet, in form as palpable   40
As this which now I draw.
Thou marshall'st me the way that I was going,
And such an instrument I was to use.
Mine eyes are made the fools o' th' other senses,
Or else worth all the rest. I see thee still;   45
And on thy blade and dudgeon gouts of blood,
Which was not so before. There's no such thing:
It is the bloody business which informs
Thus to mine eyes. Now o'er the one half world
Nature seems dead, and wicked dreams abuse   50
The curtain'd sleep; witchcraft celebrates
Pale Heccat's off'rings; and wither'd Murther,
Alarum'd by his sentinel, the wolf,
Whose howl's his watch, thus with his stealthy pace,
With Tarquin's ravishing strides, towards his design
Moves like a ghost. Thou sure and firm-set earth,
Hear not my steps, which way they walk, for fear
Thy very stones prate of my whereabout,
And take the present horror from the time,   59

36 **sensible** perceptible. 46 **dudgeon** handle. **gouts** drops. 48 **informs** gives information; takes shape (?). 52 **Heccat's off'rings** offerings to Hecate, the classical goddess of witchcraft (the phonetic spelling of F indicates the pronunciation). 53 **alarum'd** aroused. 54 **Whose howl's his watch** N. 55 **Tarquin's** N. **strides** F *sides*. 56 **sure** F *sowre*. 57 **way they** F *they may*. 59 **present horror** i.e. silence.

Which now suits with it. Whiles I threat he lives:
Words to the heat of deeds too cold breath gives.

A bell rings.

I go, and it is done; the bell invites me.
Hear it not, Duncan, for it is a knell
That summons thee to heaven or to hell. **Exit.**

SCENE 2

Enter Lady.

Lady Macbeth. That which hath made them drunk
    hath made me bold:
What hath quench'd them hath given me fire.
Hark! Peace! It was the owl that shriek'd,
The fatal bellman, which gives the stern'st good
    night.
He is about it; the doors are open; 5
And the surfeited grooms do mock their charge
With snores. I have drugg'd their possets,
That death and nature do contend about them,
Whether they live or die.
    Macbeth. [*Within.*]   Who's there? what, ho!
    Lady Macbeth. Alack! I am afraid they have
        awak'd, 10
And 'tis not done; th' attempt and not the deed
Confounds us. Hark! I laid their daggers ready;
He could not miss 'em. Had he not resembled
My father as he slept I had done't.

Enter Macbeth.

4 bellman watchman, town crier N. 7 posset a punch made of hot
milk curdled with ale or wine. 12 confounds ruins. SD Enter
Macbeth N.

My husband!

Macbeth. I have done the deed. Didst thou not hear
a noise? 15

Lady Macbeth. I heard the owl scream and the
crickets cry.

Did not you speak?

Macbeth.　　　　When?

Lady Macbeth.　　　　Now.

Macbeth.　　　　　　　　As I descended?

Lady Macbeth. Ay.

Macbeth.　　　　　Hark! Who lies i' th' second
chamber?

Lady Macbeth. Donalbain.

Macbeth. [*Looking on his hands.*] This is a sorry
sight.

Lady Macbeth. A foolish thought to say a sorry
sight. 20

Macbeth. There's one did laugh in's sleep,
And one cried 'Murther!' that they did wake each
other.
I stood and heard them; but they did say their
prayers,
And address'd them again to sleep.

Lady Macbeth. There are two lodg'd together.

Macbeth. One cried 'God bless us!' and 'Amen' the
other, 25
As they had seen me with these hangman's hands.
List'ning their fear, I could not say 'Amen,'
When they did say 'God bless us!'

Lady Macbeth.　　　　　　　Consider it not
so deeply.

Macbeth. But wherefore could not I pronounce
'Amen'?

26 As as if. **hangman** used loosely for 'executioner.'

28

I had most need of blessing, and 'Amen'   30
Stuck in my throat.
   Lady Macbeth.   These deeds must not be thought
After these ways; so, it will make us mad.
   Macbeth. Methought I heard a voice cry 'Sleep no
     more!
Macbeth does murther Sleep,' the innocent Sleep,
Sleep that knits up the ravel'd sleave of care,   35
The death of each day's life, sore labor's bath,
Balm of hurt minds, great nature's second course,
Chief nourisher in life's feast,—
   Lady Macbeth.   What do you mean?
   Macbeth. Still it cried, 'Sleep no more!' to all the
     house;   39
'Glamis hath murther'd sleep, and therefore Cawdor
Shall sleep no more: Macbeth shall sleep no more!'
   Lady Macbeth. Who was it that thus cried? Why
     worthy thane,
You do unbend your noble strength to think
So brainsickly of things. Go get some water,
And wash this filthy witness from your hand.   45
Why did you bring these daggers from the place?
They must lie there. Go carry them, and smear
The sleepy grooms with blood.
   Macbeth.   I'll go no more.
I am afraid to think what I have done;
Look on't again I dare not.
   Lady Macbeth.   Infirm of purpose!   50
Give me the daggers. The sleeping and the dead
Are but as pictures; 'tis the eye of childhood

---

35 **knits** ties, fastens. **ravel'd** frayed, disintegrated. **sleave** slender
filament of silk obtained by separating (sleaving) thicker thread.
37 **second course** i.e. the main course of an Elizabethan dinner.
43 **unbend** relax.

That fears a painted devil. If he do bleed,
I'll gild the faces of the grooms withal,
For it must seem their guilt.   *Exit. Knock within.*
 Macbeth.   Whence is that knock-
  ing?   55
How is't with me, when every noise appalls me?
What hands are here? Ha! they pluck out mine eyes.
Will all great Neptune's ocean wash this blood
Clean from my hand? No, this my hand will rather
The multitudinous seas incarnardine,   60
Making the green one red.

     Enter Lady.

 Lady Macbeth. My hands are of your color, but I
  shame
To wear a heart so white.—   *Knock.*
I hear a knocking at the south entry.
Retire we to our chamber.   65
A little water clears us of this deed.
How easy is it, then! Your constancy
Hath left you unattended.   *Knock.*
      Hark! more knocking.
Get on your night-gown, lest occasion call us,
And show us to be watchers. Be not lost 70
So poorly in your thoughts.
 Macbeth. To know my deed   *Knock.*
     'Twere best not know
  myself.
Wake Duncan with thy knocking!
        I would thou
  couldst!   *Exeunt.*

60 incarnardine incarnadine, redden. 67–8 constancy . . . unattended firmness has abandoned you. 69 night-gown dressing
gown. 71 poorly feebly.
  30

SCENE 3

Enter a Porter. Knocking within.

Porter. Here's a knocking, indeed! If a man were porter of hell-gate he should have old turning the key. (*Knock.*) Knock, knock, knock! Who's there, i' th' name of Belzebub? Here's a farmer that hang'd himself on th' expectation of plenty. Come in, time-server; have napkins enow about you; here you'll sweat for't. (*Knock.*) Knock, knock! Who's there, in th' other devil's name? Faith, here's an equivocator, that could swear in both the scales against either scale; who committed treason enough for God's sake, yet could not equivocate to heaven. O, come in, equivocator! (*Knock.*) Knock, knock, knock! Who's there? Faith, here's an English tailor come hither for stealing out of a French hose. Come in, tailor; here you may roast your goose. (*Knock.*) Knock, knock! Never at quiet! What are you? But this place is too cold for hell. I'll devil-porter it no further. I had thought to have let in some of all professions, that go the primrose way to th' ever-lasting bonfire. (*Knock.*) Anon, anon! I pray you, remember the porter. [*Opens the gate.*]

Enter Macduff and Lennox.

Macduff. Was it so late, friend, ere you went to bed, that you do lie so late? 23

2 should would. old plenty of (colloquial). 4 Belzebub Beelzebub.
farmer N. 5–6 come in, time-server F *Come in time* N. 6 napkins
handkerchiefs. enow enough. 8 equivocator N. 14 stealing . . .
hose N. 15 goose smoothing iron N. 20 anon right away. 22–6
Was . . . things F prints as verse.

Porter. Faith, sir, we were carousing till the second cock; and drink, sir, is a great provoker of three things.

Macduff. What three things does drink especially provoke? 28

Porter. Marry, sir, nose-painting, sleep, and urine. Lechery, sir, it provokes, and unprovokes: it provokes the desire, but it takes away the performance. Therefore much drink may be said to be an equivocator with Lechery: it makes him, and it mars him; it sets him on, and it takes him off; it persuades him, and disheartens him; makes him stand to, and not stand to; in conclusion, equivocates him in a sleep, and, giving him the lie, leaves him. 37

Macduff. I believe drink gave thee the lie last night.

Porter. That it did, sir, i' the very throat on me; but I requited him for his lie; and, I think, being too strong for him, though he took up my legs sometime, yet I made a shift to cast him. 42

Enter Macbeth.

Macduff. Is thy master stirring?
Our knocking has awak'd him; here he comes.

Lennox. Good morrow, noble sir.

Macbeth.   Good morrow, both. 45

Macduff. Is the king stirring, worthy thane?

Macbeth.   Not yet.

---

24 **second cock** i.e. about 3 A.M. 41 **took up my legs** got my feet off the ground (as in wrestling). 42 **made a shift** contrived. 42 **cast** throw; also 'vomit.' SD **Enter Macbeth** N.

Macduff. He did command me to call timely on him;
I have almost slipp'd the hour.
Macbeth.   I'll bring you to him.
Macduff. I know this is a joyful trouble to you;
But yet 'tis one.   50
Macbeth. The labor we delight in physics pain.
This is the door.
Macduff.   I'll make so bold to call,
For 'tis my limited service.   *Exit Macduff.*
Lennox. Goes the king hence today?
Macbeth.   He does; he did
          appoint so.
Lennox. The night has been unruly.   55
Where we lay, our chimneys were blown down,
And, as they say, lamentings heard i' th' air,
Strange screams of death,
And prophesying with accents terrible
Of dire combustion and confus'd events   60
New hatch'd to th' woeful time.
The obscure bird clamor'd the livelong night.
Some say the earth was feverous, and did shake.
Macbeth. 'Twas a rough night.   64
Lennox. My young remembrance cannot parallel
A fellow to it.

Enter Macduff.

Macduff.   O horror! horror! horror!
Tongue nor heart cannot conceive nor name thee!
Macbeth.⎫
Lennox. ⎬ What's the matter?
Macduff. Confusion now hath made his masterpiece!

48 slipp'd missed. 51 physics cures. 53 limited appointed. 55–63
The night . . . shake N. 60 combustion tumult, disorder. 62 obscure bird bird of darkness, the owl. 66 fellow equal.

Most sacrilegious murther hath broke ope   70
The Lord's anointed temple, and stole thence
The life o' th' building!
   Macbeth.   What is't you say? the life?
   Lennox. Mean you his majesty?
   Macduff. Approach the chamber, and destroy your
     sight
With a new Gorgon. Do not bid me speak.   75
See, and then speak yourselves.
                    Exeunt Macbeth and Lennox.
                      Awake! awake!
Ring the alarum-bell. Murther and treason!
Banquo and Donalbain! Malcolm, awake!
Shake off this downy sleep, death's counterfeit,
And look on death itself! up, up, and see   80
The great doom's image! Malcolm, Banquo,
As from your graves rise up, and walk like sprites,
To countenance this horror! Ring the bell.

Bell rings. Enter Lady.

   Lady Macbeth. What's the business,
That such a hideous trumpet calls to parley   85
The sleepers of the house? speak, speak!
   Macduff.   O gentle
     lady,
'Tis not for you to hear what I can speak;
The repetition in a woman's ear
Would murther as it fell.

Enter Banquo.

71 **Lord's anointed temple** anointed body of the king. 75 **Gorgon**
a monster whose aspect turned the beholder to stone. 81 **great
doom's image** likeness of doomsday. 82 **sprites** spirits. 83 **countenance** face (?) or accord with (?).

O Banquo, Banquo,
Our royal master's murther'd!
 Lady Macbeth.   Woe, alas! 90
What, in our house?
 Banquo.   Too cruel anywhere.
Dear Duff, I prithee contradict thyself,
And say it is not so.

Enter Macbeth and Lennox.

 Macbeth. Had I but died an hour before this chance,
I had liv'd a blessed time; for, from this instant 95
There's nothing serious in mortality:
All is but toys; renown and grace is dead,
The wine of life is drawn, and the mere lees
Is left this vault to brag of.

Enter Malcolm and Donalbain.

 Donalbain. What is amiss?
 Macbeth.   You are, and do not
 know't: 100
The spring, the head, the fountain of your blood
Is stopp'd; the very source of it is stopp'd.
 Macduff. Your royal father's murther'd.
 Malcolm.   O, by
 whom?
 Lennox. Those of his chamber, as it seem'd, had
 done't. 104
Their hands and faces were all badg'd with blood;
So were their daggers, which unwip'd we found
Upon their pillows. They star'd and were distracted,
No man's life was to be trusted with them.

SD Enter Macbeth and Lennox N. 96 mortality mortal life.
97 toys trifles. 99 vault N. 105 badg'd marked with.

Macbeth. O, yet I do repent me of my fury,
That I did kill them.
 Macduff.   Wherefore did you so? 110
 Macbeth. Who can be wise, amaz'd, temp'rate and
  furious,
Loyal and neutral, in a moment? No man.
Th' expedition of my violent love
Outrun the pauser, reason. Here lay Duncan,
His silver skin lac'd with his golden blood; 115
And his gash'd stabs look'd like a breach in nature
For ruin's wasteful entrance; there, the murtherers,
Steep'd in the colors of their trade; their daggers
Unmannerly breech'd with gore. Who could refrain,
That had a heart to love, and in that heart 120
Courage to make's love known?
 Lady Macbeth.   Help me hence, ho!
 Macduff. Look to the lady.
 Malcolm. [*Aside to Donalbain.*] Why do we hold
  our tongues,
That most may claim this argument for ours?
 Donalbain. [*Aside to Malcolm.*] What should be
  spoken here,
Where our fate, hid in an auger-hole, 125
May rush and seize us? Let's away.
Our tears are not yet brew'd.
 Malcolm. [*Aside to Donalbain.*] Nor our strong
  sorrow
Upon the foot of motion.
 Banquo.   Look to the lady.
      [*Lady Macbeth is carried out.*]

113 **expedition** speed. 114 **Outrun** outran. 115 **lac'd** decorated in a
lacy pattern. 119 **Unmannerly . . . gore** N. 123 **argument** subject. 125–6 **where . . . seize us** N. 125 **auger-hole** i.e. a small
hole. 127–9 **Our tears . . . motion** N.

And when we have our naked frailties hid,
That suffer in exposure, let us meet,   130
And question this most bloody piece of work,
To know it further. Fears and scruples shake us.
In the great hand of God I stand, and thence
Against the undivulg'd pretence I fight
Of treasonous malice.

Macduff.   And so do I.
All.   So all.   135
Macbeth. Let's briefly put on manly readiness,
And meet i' th' hall together.

All.   Well contented.

          Exeunt [all but Malcolm and Donalbain.]
Malcolm. What will you do? Let's not consort with
    them.
To show an unfelt sorrow is an office   139
Which the false man does easy. I'll to England.

Donalbain. To Ireland, I; our separated fortune
Shall keep us both the safer. Where we are,
There's daggers in men's smiles; the near in blood,
The nearer bloody.

Malcolm.   This murtherous shaft that's
    shot
Hath not yet lighted, and our safest way   145
Is to avoid the aim. Therefore, to horse!
And let us not be dainty of leave-taking,
But shift away. There's warrant in that theft
Which steals itself when there's no mercy left.

                                    Exeunt.

---

129 **naked frailties** N. 134 **pretence** design. 136 **briefly quickly.**
143 **near** nearer. 147 **dainty of** particular about. 148 **shift** steal.
warrant justification.

SCENE 4

Enter Ross with an Old Man.

Old Man. Threescore and ten I can remember well,
Within the volume of which time I have seen
Hours dreadful and things strange, but this sore
    night
Hath trifled former knowings.
Ross.   Ha! good father,   4
Thou seest the heavens, as troubled with man's act,
Threatens his bloody stage. By th' clock 'tis day,
And yet dark night strangles the traveling lamp.
Is't night's predominance, or the day's shame,
That darkness does the face of earth entomb,   9
When living light should kiss it?
Old Man.   'Tis unnatural,
Even like the deed that's done. On Tuesday last,
A falcon, tow'ring in her pride of place,
Was by a mousing owl hawk'd at and kill'd.
Ross. And Duncan's horses—a thing most strange
    and certain—,
Beauteous and swift, the minions of their race,   15
Turn'd wild in nature, broke their stalls, flung out,
Contending 'gainst obedience, as they would
Make war with mankind.
Old Man.   'Tis said they eat each
    other.

---

4 trifled made trifles of. **5–20 thou . . . upon't** see II.3.55–63 N.
6 Threatens threaten. **stage** N. **7 lamp** i.e. the sun. **12 tow'ring
. . . place** N. **13 mousing** i.e. that normally flies near to the
ground. **15 minions** darlings, i.e. best. **18 eat** ate.

Ross. They did so, to th' amazement of mine eyes,
That look'd upon't.

Enter Macduff.

Here comes the good Macduff.
How goes the world, sir, now?
   Macduff.   Why see you not?
   Ross. Is't known who did this more than bloody
deed?
   Macduff. Those that Macbeth hath slain.
   Ross.   Alas, the
   day!
What good could they pretend?
   Macduff.   They were
   suborn'd.
Malcolm and Donalbain, the king's two sons,   25
Are stol'n away and fled, which puts upon them
Suspicion of the deed.
   Ross.   'Gainst nature still!
Thriftless ambition, that will ravin up
Thine own life's means! Then 'tis most like
The sovereignty will fall upon Macbeth.   30
   Macduff. He is already nam'd, and gone to Scone
To be invested.
   Ross.   Where is Duncan's body?
   Macduff. Carried to Colmekill,
The sacred storehouse of his predecessors   34
And guardian of their bones.
   Ross.   Will you to Scone?
   Macduff. No, cousin, I'll to Fife.

---

24 pretend intend. suborn'd induced to commit a crime. 28 ravin
up swallow greedily. 32 invested robed and crowned. 33 Colmekill
island in the Hebrides now called Iona.

Ross.   Well, I will
   thither.
Macduff. Well, may you see things well done there.
   Adieu!
Lest our old robes sit easier than our new!
   Ross. Farewell, father.
   Old Man. God's benison go with you, and with
      those   40
That would make good of bad, and friends of foes!
                                          Exeunt omnes.

40 **benison** blessing.

Act III

SCENE 1

Enter Banquo.

Banquo. Thou hast it now: king, Cawdor, Glamis,
    all,
As the weyard women promis'd; and I fear
Thou play'dst most foully for't; yet it was said
It should not stand in thy posterity,
But that myself should be the root and father   5
Of many kings. If there come truth from them—
As upon thee, Macbeth, their speeches shine—
Why, by the verities on thee made good,
May they not be my oracles as well,
And set me up in hope? But hush, no more.   10

Sennet sounded. Enter Macbeth, as king; Lady;
    Lennox, Ross, Lords, and Attendants.

Macbeth. Here's our chief guest.
Lady Macbeth.   If he had been for-
    gotten,
It had been as a gap in our great feast,
And all-thing unbecoming.
Macbeth. Tonight we hold a solemn supper, sir,
And I'll request your presence.
Banquo.   Let your highness

SD **Sennet** trumpet call. 13 **all-thing** wholly. 14 **solemn** formal,
ceremonious; see III.4.36–8.

Command upon me, to the which my duties 16
Are with a most indissoluble tie
Forever knit.

Macbeth. Ride you this afternoon?

Banquo.   Ay, my good
lord.

Macbeth. We should have else desir'd your good
advice— 20
Which still hath been both grave and prosperous—
In this day's council; but we'll take tomorrow.
Is't far you ride?

Banquo. As far, my lord, as will fill up the time
'Twixt this and supper. Go not my horse the better,
I must become a borrower of the night 26
For a dark hour or twain.

Macbeth.   Fail not our feast.

Banquo. My lord, I will not.

Macbeth. We hear our bloody cousins are bestow'd
In England and in Ireland, not confessing 30
Their cruel parricide, filling their hearers
With strange invention. But of that tomorrow,
When therewithal we shall have cause of state
Craving us jointly. Hie you to horse. Adieu, 34
Till you return at night. Goes Fleance with you?

Banquo. Ay, my good lord; our time does call
upon's.

Macbeth. I wish your horses swift and sure of foot;
And so I do commend you to their backs.
Farewell.   *Exit Banquo.*
Let every man be master of his time 40

17 indissoluble stressed — ´ — ˋ —. 21 still . . . prosperous
has always been weighty and profitable. 25 Go . . . better N.
33 cause of state public business. 34 craving us jointly demanding
our joint attention.

Till seven at night;
To make society the sweeter welcome,
We will keep ourself till suppertime alone.
While then, God be with you.
   Exeunt [all but Macbeth and a Servant.]
      Sirrah, a word with

 you.
Attend those men our pleasure?
 Servant.   They are, my lord,
Without the palace gate.
 Macbeth.   Bring them before us. 46
         Exit Servant.

To be thus is nothing, but to be safely thus.
Our fears in Banquo stick deep,
And in his royalty of nature reigns
That which would be fear'd. 'Tis much he dares, 50
And to that dauntless temper of his mind
He hath a wisdom that doth guide his valor
To act in safety. There is none but he
Whose being I do fear; and under him
My genius is rebuk'd, as it is said 55
Mark Antony's was by Caesar. He chid the sisters
When first they put the name of king upon me,
And bade them speak to him. Then, prophet-like,
They hail'd him father to a line of kings.
Upon my head they plac'd a fruitless crown, 60
And put a barren scepter in my gripe,
Thence to be wrench'd with an unlineal hand,
No son of mine succeeding. If't be so,
For Banquo's issue have I fil'd my mind; 64

42–7 To make . . . safely thus N. 42 sweeter more sweetly.
44 While then till then. 47 but unless. 55–6 My genius . . .
Caesar N. 55 genius guardian spirit. rebuk'd cowed. 64 fil'd
defiled.

For them the gracious Duncan have I murther'd;
Put rancors in the vessel of my peace
Only for them; and mine eternal jewel
Given to the common enemy of man,
To make them kings, the seeds of Banquo kings!
Rather than so, come Fate into the list,   70
And champion me to th' utterance!

                                        Who's there?

Enter Servant and two Murtherers.

Now go to the door, and stay there till we call.
                                        Exit Servant.
Was it not yesterday we spoke together?
   Murtherers. It was, so please your highness.
   Macbeth.   Well
      then,
Now have you consider'd of my speeches;   75
Know that it was he, in the times past,
Which held you so under fortune,
Which you thought had been our innocent self.
This I made good to you in our last conference;
Pass'd in probation with you   80
How you were borne in hand, how cross'd,
The instruments, who wrought with them,
And all things else that might to half a soul
And to a notion craz'd say, 'Thus did Banquo.'
   1 Murtherer. You made it known to us.   85

66 rancors bitter enmities. vessel of my peace peace is compared
to a liquid in a container. 67 jewel i.e. soul. 70 list lists. 71
champion fight. utterance uttermost. Who's there? a customary
phrase to summon the servant. 75 have you you have. 76 Know
i.e. now you know. 77 under fortune in distress. 79 made good
proved. 80 Pass'd in probation went over the proofs. 81 borne in
hand deceived. 84 notion mind.

Macbeth. I did so; and went further, which is now
Our point of second meeting. Do you find
Your patience so predominant in your nature
That you can let this go? Are you so gospel'd
To pray for this good man and for his issue,   90
Whose heavy hand hath bow'd you to the grave
And beggar'd yours forever?

    1 Murtherer.   We are men, my liege.

  Macbeth. Ay, in the catalogue ye go for men,
As hounds and greyhounds, mongrels, spaniels, curs,
Shoughs, waterrugs, and demi-wolves, are clipt   95
All by the name of dogs. The valued file
Distinguishes the swift, the slow, the subtle,
The housekeeper, the hunter, every one
According to the gift which bounteous nature
Hath in him clos'd; whereby he does receive   100
Particular addition, from the bill
That writes them all alike; and so of men.
Now, if you have a station in the file,
Not i' th' worst rank of manhood, say't;
And I will put that business in your bosoms,   105
Whose execution takes your enemy off,
Grapples you to the heart and love of us,
Who wear our health but sickly in his life,
Which in his death were perfect.

    2 Murtherer.   I am one, my liege,
Whom the vile blows and buffets of the world   110
Hath so incens'd that I am reckless what

---

89 **gospel'd** so filled with Christian forgiveness. 95 **Shoughs** pronounced 'shocks'; shag-haired dogs. **waterrugs** shaggy water dogs. **clipt** called. 96 **valued file** list in which value is recorded. 101 **addition** title. 101–2 **from . . . alike** i.e. to distinguish him from the others in the general category of dogs. 108 **in** during. 111 **hath** have.

I do to spite the world.

  1 Murtherer.   And I another,
So weary with disasters, tugg'd with Fortune,
That I would set my life on any chance,
To mend it or be rid on't.

  Macbeth.   Both of you   115
Know Banquo was your enemy.

  Murtherers.   True, my lord.

  Macbeth. So is he mine; and in such bloody distance
That every minute of his being thrusts
Against my near'st of life; and though I could
With barefac'd power sweep him from my sight
And bid my will avouch it, yet I must not,   121
For certain friends that are both his and mine,
Whose loves I may not drop, but wail his fall
Who I myself struck down. And thence it is
That I to your assistance do make love,   125
Masking the business from the common eye
For sundry weighty reasons.

  2 Murtherer.   We shall my lord,
Perform what you command us.

  1 Murtherer.   Though our lives—

  Macbeth. Your spirits shine through you. Within this hour at most
I will advise you where to plant yourselves,   130
Acquaint you with the perfect spy o' th' time,
The moment on't, for't must be done tonight,
And something from the palace; always thought

---

113 **tugg'd with** pulled about by. 117 **distance** enmity. 119 **near'st of life** most vital parts. 121 **avouch** justify. 122 **For** on account of. 123 **but wail** but I must wail. 130 **advise** inform. 131 **perfect spy** exact indication (literally, 'observation') N. 132 **on't** for it. 133 **something** a little way. **always thought** i.e. it must be kept in mind.

That I require a clearness; and with him,
To leave no rubs nor botches in the work, 135
Fleance his son, that keeps him company,
Whose absence is no less material to me
Than is his father's, must embrace the fate
Of that dark hour. Resolve yourselves apart;
I'll come to you anon.
 Murtherers. We are resolv'd, my lord. 140
 Macbeth. I'll call upon you straight. Abide within.
        [Exeunt Murtherers.]
It is concluded. Banquo, thy soul's flight,
If it find heaven, must find it out tonight.
          [Exit.]

SCENE 2

Enter Macbeth's Lady and a Servant.

 Lady Macbeth. Is Banquo gone from court?
 Servant. Ay, madam, but returns again tonight.
 Lady Macbeth. Say to the king, I would attend his
  leisure
For a few words.
 Servant. Madam, I will.   *Exit.*
 Lady Macbeth.   Nought's had, all's
  spent,
Where our desire is got without content. 5
'Tis safer to be that which we destroy
Than by destruction dwell in doubtful joy.

Enter Macbeth.

134 **clearness** freedom from suspicion. 135 **rubs nor botches**
roughness nor clumsy patching. 139 **Resolve yourselves** make up
your minds.

47

How now, my lord? Why do you keep alone,
Of sorriest fancies your companions making, 9
Using those thoughts which should indeed have died
With them they think on? Things without all remedy
Should be without regard: what's done is done.

Macbeth. We have scorch'd the snake, not kill'd it:
She'll close and be herself, whilst our poor malice
Remains in danger of her former tooth. 15
But let the frame of things disjoint, both the worlds
suffer,
Ere we will eat our meal in fear, and sleep
In the affliction of these terrible dreams
That shake us nightly. Better be with the dead,
Whom we, to gain our peace, have sent to peace, 20
Than on the torture of the mind to lie
In restless ecstasy.
Duncan is in his grave;
After life's fitful fever he sleeps well. 24
Treason has done his worst. Nor steel, nor poison,
Malice domestic, foreign levy, nothing
Can touch him further.

Lady Macbeth. Come on:
Gentle my lord, sleek o'er your rugged looks;
Be bright and jovial among your guests tonight.

Macbeth. So shall I, love, and so, I pray, be you.
Let your remembrance apply to Banquo; 31
Present him eminence, both with eye and tongue—
Unsafe the while that we must lave
Our honors in these flattering streams,
And make our faces vizards to our hearts, 35

13 scorch'd slashed as with a knife N. 16 frame of things disjoint
structure of the universe fall to pieces. both the worlds i.e. celes-
tial and terrestrial. 22 ecstasy frenzy. 28 sleek smooth. 31
remembrance read 'rememberance.' 32 Present him eminence do
him honor. 33 Unsafe i.e. though we are unsafe. 35 vizards masks.

Disguising what they are.

Lady Macbeth.　　　　You must leave this.

Macbeth. O, full of scorpions is my mind, dear
　　wife!
Thou know'st that Banquo and his Fleance lives.

Lady Macbeth. But in them nature's copy's not
　　eterne.

Macbeth. There's comfort yet; they are assailable;
Then be thou jocund. Ere the bat hath flown　　41
His cloister'd flight, ere to black Heccat's summons
The shard-borne beetle with his drowsy hums
Hath rung night's yawning peal, there shall be done
A deed of dreadful note.

Lady Macbeth.　　　　What's to be done?　　45

Macbeth. Be innocent of the knowledge, dearest
　　chuck,
Till thou applaud the deed. Come, seeling night,
Scarf up the tender eye of pitiful day,
And with thy bloody and invisible hand
Cancel and tear to pieces that great bond　　50
Which keeps me pale! Light thickens, and the crow
Makes wing to th' rooky wood.
Good things of day begin to droop and drowse,
Whiles night's black agents to their preys do rouse.
Thou marvell'st at my words; but hold thee still;
Things bad begun make strong themselves by ill.
So prithee go with me.　　　　　　　*Exeunt.*

38 **lives** live. 39 **copy** pattern N. 43 **shard-borne** N. 46 **chuck**
familiar term of endearment. 47 **seeling** sewing up the eyelids
(a term from falconry). 50 **bond** N. 52 **rooky** filled with rooks.

SCENE 3

Enter three Murtherers.

1 Murtherer. But who did bid thee join with us?

3 Murtherer.   Macbeth.

2 Murtherer. He needs not our mistrust, since he
    delivers
Our offices and what we have to do
To the direction just.

1 Murtherer.   Then stand with us.   4
The west yet glimmers with some streaks of day.
Now spurs the lated traveler apace
To gain the timely inn, and near approaches
The subject of our watch.

3 Murtherer.   Hark! I hear horses.

Banquo within. Give us a light there, ho!

2 Murtherer.   Then 'tis
    he;
The rest that are within the note of expectation
Already are i' th' court.

1 Murtherer.   His horses go about.   11

3 Murtherer. Almost a mile; but he does usually,
So all men do, from hence to th' palace gate
Make it their walk.

Enter Banquo and Fleance with a torch.

2 Murtherer.   A light, a light!

3 Murtherer.   'Tis he.

---

2 **He needs not our mistrust** i.e. we need not distrust him (the
third murderer). 2 **delivers** reports. 3 **offices** duties. 4 **To the
direction** according to the instructions (of Macbeth). 10 **note of
expectation** list of expected guests. SD **Enter Banquo and Fleance**
See II.3.42 SD **N.**

1 Murtherer. Stand to't.   15
Banquo. It will be rain tonight.
1 Murtherer.   Let it come down,
                    [*Strikes out light; stabs Banquo.*]
Banquo. O, treachery! Fly, good Fleance, fly, fly,
    fly!
Thou mayst revenge. O slave!
                              [*Dies. Fleance escapes.*]
3 Murtherer. Who did strike out the light?
1 Murtherer.   Was't
    not the way?   19
3 Murtherer. There's but one down; the son is fled.
2 Murtherer.   We have lost
Best half of our affair.
1 Murtherer. Well, let's away, and say how much
    is done.   *Exeunt.*

SCENE 4

Banquet prepared. Enter Macbeth, Lady, Ross,
    Lennox, Lords and Attendants.

Macbeth. You know your own degrees; sit down.
At first and last, the hearty welcome.
Lords. Thanks to your majesty.
Macbeth. Ourself will mingle with society
And play the humble host.   5
Our hostess keeps her state, but in best time
We will require her welcome.
Lady Macbeth. Pronounce it for me, sir, to all our
    friends,
For my heart speaks they are welcome.

1 degrees ranks. 2 At first and last once for all. 4-6 Ourself . . .
state N. 7 require request.

Enter First Murtherer [to the door].

Macbeth. See, they encounter thee with their hearts'
    thanks.   10
Both sides are even; here I'll sit i' th' midst.
Be large in mirth; anon, we'll drink a measure
The table round. [*Approaching the door.*] There's
    blood upon thy face.

Murtherer. 'Tis Banquo's, then.   14

Macbeth. 'Tis better thee without than he within.
Is he dispatch'd?

Murtherer. My lord, his throat is cut; that I did
    for him.

Macbeth. Thou art the best o' th' cut-throats;
Yet he's good that did the like for Fleance:
If thou didst it, thou art the nonpareil.   20

Murtherer. Most royal sir—
                         Fleance is 'scap'd.

Macbeth. Then comes my fit again; I had else been
    perfect;
Whole as the marble, founded as the rock,
As broad and general as the casing air.   24
But now I am cabin'd, cribb'd, confin'd, bound in
To saucy doubts and fears. But Banquo's safe?

Murtherer. Ay, my good lord; safe in a ditch he
    bides,
With twenty trenched gashes on his head;
The least a death to nature.

Macbeth.   Thanks for that.
There the grown serpent lies; the worm that's fled

11 **Both sides are even** i.e. there are equal numbers on both sides
of the table. 12 **measure** large goblet. 13 **Approaching the door** N.
15 **thee . . . within** outside you than inside him. 20 **nonpareil**
unequaled one. 24 **broad and general** free and unconfined. **casing**
surrounding. 28 **trenched** cut.

Hath nature that in time will venom breed,   31
No teeth for th' present. Get thee gone; tomorrow
We'll hear ourselves again.   *Exit Murderer.*
  Lady Macbeth.   My royal lord,
You do not give the cheer. The feast is sold
That is not often vouch'd, while 'tis a-making;   35
'Tis given with welcome. To feed were best at home;
From thence, the sauce to meat is ceremony;
Meeting were bare without it.

     Enter the Ghost of Banquo, and sits in
            Macbeth's place.

  Macbeth.   Sweet remembrancer!
Now good digestion wait on appetite,   39
And health on both!
  Lennox.   May't please your highness sit?
  Macbeth. Here had we now our country's honor
    roof'd,
Were the grac'd person of our Banquo present;
Who may I rather challenge for unkindness
Than pity for mischance!
  Ross.   His absence, sir,   44
Lays blame upon his promise. Please't your highness
To grace us with your royal company?
  Macbeth. The table's full.
  Lennox.   Here is a place reserv'd,
    sir.
  Macbeth.   Where?
  Lennox. Here, my good lord. What is't that moves
    your highness?

33 hear ourselves confer. 34–6 The feast . . . welcome N. SD
Enter . . . Banquo N. 38 remembrancer one who reminds another N. 41 had we we should have. 41 honor noblemen. roof'd
under one roof.

Macbeth. Which of you have done this?

Lords.   What, my
good lord?   49

Macbeth. Thou canst not say I did it; never shake
Thy gory locks at me.

Ross. Gentlemen, rise; his highness is not well.

Lady Macbeth. Sit, worthy friends. My lord is
often thus,
And hath been from his youth. Pray you, keep seat;
The fit is momentary; upon a thought   55
He will again be well. If much you note him
You shall offend him and extend his passion;
Feed and regard him not. Are you a man?

Macbeth. Ay, and a bold one, that dare look on
that
Which might appall the divel.

Lady Macbeth.   O proper stuff!   60
This is the very painting of your fear;
This is the air-drawn dagger which you said
Led you to Duncan. O, these flaws and starts—
Impostors to true fear—would well become
A woman's story at a winter's fire,   65
Authoriz'd by her grandam. Shame itself!
Why do you make such faces? When all's done
You look but on a stool.

Macbeth.   Prithee, see there!
Behold! look! lo! how say you?   69
Why, what care I? If thou canst nod, speak too.
If charnel houses and our graves must send
Those that we bury back, our monuments

---

55 upon a thought in a moment. **57 extend** increase. **63 flaws** outbursts. **64 Impostors** false pretenders. **66 Authoriz'd** stressed
— $-$ —; vouched for. **68 stool** N. **71-3 If charnel houses** . . .
kites N. **charnel houses** repositories for bones.

Shall be the maws of kites.   [*Exit Ghost.*]
   Lady Macbeth.   What! quite unmann'd in
    folly?
   Macbeth. If I stand here, I saw him.
   Lady Macbeth.   Fie, for
    shame!
   Macbeth. Blood hath been shed ere now, i' th' olden
    time,   75
Ere humane statute purg'd the gentle weal;
Ay, and since too, murthers have been perform'd
Too terrible for the ear. The times has been,
That, when the brains were out, the man would die,
And there an end. But now they rise again,   80
With twenty mortal murthers on their crowns,
And push us from our stools. This is more strange
Than such a murther is.
   Lady Macbeth.   My worthy lord,
Your noble friends do lack you.
   Macbeth.   I do forget.
Do not muse at me, my most worthy friends;   85
I have a strange infirmity, which is nothing
To those that know me. Come, love and health to all;
Then, I'll sit down. Give me some wine; fill full.

Enter Ghost.

I drink to th' general joy o' th' whole table,
And to our dear friend Banquo, whom we miss.   90
Would he were here! to all, and him, we thirst,
And all to all.
   Lords.   Our duties, and the pledge.

76 **humane** stressed ´ —; both 'human' and 'humane.' **gentle
weal** civilized state. 78 **has** have. 81 **murthers** i.e. wounds. 85
muse wonder. SD **Enter Ghost** see III.4.38SD N. 91 **thirst** are
eager to drink. 92 **all to all** all drink to all.

Macbeth. Avaunt, and quit my sight! Let the eartl.
 hide thee!
Thy bones are marrowless, thy blood is cold;
Thou hast no speculation in those eyes   9₁
Which thou dost glare with.
 Lady Macbeth.   Think of this, good
 peers,
But as a thing of custom. 'Tis no other;
Only it spoils the pleasure of the time.
 Macbeth. What man dare, I dare.
Approach thou like the rugged Russian bear,   100
The arm'd rhinoceros, or th' Hyrcan tiger;
Take any shape but that, and my firm nerves
Shall never tremble. Or be alive again,
And dare me to the desart with thy sword;
If trembling I inhabit then, protest me   105
The baby of a girl. Hence, horrible shadow!
Unreal mock'ry, hence!   [*Exit Ghost.*]
                    Why, so; being gone
I am a man again. Pray you, sit still.
 Lady Macbeth. You have displac'd the mirth, broke
 the good meeting
With most admir'd disorder.
 Macbeth.   Can such things be
And overcome us like a summer's cloud,   111
Without our special wonder? You make me strange
Even to the disposition that I owe,
When now I think you can behold such sights,
And keep the natural ruby of your cheeks,   115

95 speculation comprehending vision. 97 of custom usual. 1⁰
Hyrcan Hyrcanian N. 102 that i.e. of Banquo. nerves sinew
104 desart desert, i.e. any solitary place. 105 inhabit live, co
tinue to live. protest proclaim. 106 The baby of a girl a baby girl.
109 displac'd banished. 110 admir'd wondered at. 111 overcome
pass over. 112–13 You . . . owe N.

Loves for his own ends, not for you.
But make amends now. Get you gone,
And at the pit of Acheron   15
Meet me i' th' morning. Thither he
Will come to know his destiny.
Your vessels and your spells provide,
Your charms and every thing beside.
I am for th' air; this night I'll spend   20
Unto a dismal and a fatal end.
Great business must be wrought ere noon.
Upon the corner of the moon
There hangs a vap'rous drop profound;
I'll catch it ere it come to ground;   25
And that distill'd by magic sleights
Shall raise such artificial sprites
As by the strength of their illusion
Shall draw him on to his confusion.
He shall spurn fate, scorn death, and bear   30
His hopes 'bove wisdom, grace, and fear;
And you all know security
Is mortals' chiefest enemy.
              Music and a song. Sing within,
                'Come away, come away,' etc.
Hark! I am call'd; my little spirit, see,
Sits in a foggy cloud, and stays for me.   35
                              [*Exit Heccat.*]
  1 Witch. Come, let's make haste; she'll soon be
     back again.   *Exeunt.*

15 Acheron a river of Hades. 27 **artificial** cunning, well-contrived.
sprites spirits. 29 **confusion** ruin. SD **Sing within** N. 34–5 **Hark
. . . for me** N.

SCENE 6

Enter Lennox and another Lord.

Lennox. My former speeches have but hit your
    thoughts,
Which can interpret farther. Only I say
Things have been strangely borne. The gracious
    Duncan
Was pitied of Macbeth. Marry, he was dead!
And the right valiant Banquo walk'd too late;   5
Whom you may say—if't please you—Fleance kill'd,
For Fleance fled. Men must not walk too late.
Who cannot want the thought how monstrous
It was for Malcolm and for Donalbain
To kill their gracious father? Damned fact!   10
How it did grieve Macbeth! Did he not straight
In pious rage the two delinquents tear,
That were the slaves of drink and thralls of sleep?
Was not that nobly done? Ay, and wisely too;
For 'twould have anger'd any heart alive   15
To hear the men deny't. So that I say
He has borne all things well; and I do think
That, had he Duncan's sons under his key—
As, and't please heaven, he shall not—they should
    find
What 'twere to kill a father; so should Fleance.   20
But, peace! for from broad words, and 'cause he
    fail'd

Scene 6 N. 1 **hit** coincided with. 3 **borne** managed. 4 **of** by. 8 **cannot want** can avoid. **monstrous** perhaps three syllables here. 19 **and** if. 21 **broad** frank, outspoken. 21–2 **fail'd/His presence** did not appear.

His presence at the tyrant's feast, I hear
Macduff lives in disgrace. Sir, can you tell
Where he bestows himself?
Lord.   The son of Duncan,
From whom this tyrant holds the due of birth,   25
Lives in the English court, and is receiv'd
Of the most pious Edward with such grace
That the malevolence of fortune nothing
Takes 'rom his high respect. Thither Macduff
Is gone to pray the holy king, upon his aid   30
To wake Northumberland and warlike Siward;
That, by the help of these (with Him above
To ratify the work) we may again
Give to our tables meat, sleep to our nights;   34
Free from our feasts and banquets bloody knives;
Do faithful homage and receive free honors,
All which we pine for now. And this report
Hath so exasperate the king that he
Prepares for some attempt of war.
Lennox.   Sent he to Mac-
    duff?   39
Lord. He did; and with an absolute 'Sir, not I'
The cloudy messenger turns me his back,
And hums, as who should say, 'You'll rue the time
That clogs me with this answer.'
Lennox.   And that well might
Advise him to a caution, t' hold what distance

24 son F *Sonnes.* 27 .Edward Edward the Confessor, King of
England (1042–66). 30 pray . . . upon his aid i.e. ask for his
assistance N. 35 Free . . . knives N. 36 free not bought by sub-
servience to the tyrant. 38 exasperate exasperated. the F *their.*
40 absolute unconditional. 'Sir, not I' Macduff's message. 41
cloudy frowning. 43 clogs hampers N.

His wisdom can provide. Some holy angel   45
Fly to the court of England and unfold
His message ere he come, that a swift blessing
May soon return to this our suffering country
Under a hand accurs'd!

   Lord.   I'll send my prayers with
   him!   *Exeunt.*

Act IV

SCENE 1

Thunder. Enter the three Witches.

1 Witch. Thrice the brinded cat hath mew'd.

2 Witch. Thrice, and once the hedge-pig whin'd.

3 Witch. Harpier cries; 'tis time, 'tis time.

1 Witch. Round about the cauldron go;

In the poison'd entrails throw.   5

Toad, that under cold stone

Days and nights has thirty-one

Swelt'red venom sleeping got,

Boil thou first i' th' charmed pot.

All. Double, double, toil and trouble;   10

Fire burn, and cauldron bubble.

2 Witch. Fillet of a fenny snake,

In the cauldron boil and bake;

Eye of newt, and toe of frog,

Wool of bat, and tongue of dog;   15

Adder's fork, and blind-worm's sting,

Lizard's leg, and howlet's wing;

For a charm of pow'rful trouble,

Like a hell-broth boil and bubble.

All. Double, double, toil and trouble;   20

1 **brinded** brindled. 2 **hedge-pig** hedgehog N. 3 **Harpier** see I.1.8–12 N. 8 **Swelt'red** 'exuded,' like sweat. 12 **Fillet** slice. **fenny** from the fens. 16 **fork** forked tongue. **blind-worm** a small lizard. 17 **howlet** owlet.

Fire burn, and cauldron bubble.

3 Witch. Scale of dragon, tooth of wolf,
Witches' mummy, maw and gulf
Of the ravin'd salt-sea shark;
Root of hemlock digg'd i' th' dark;   25
Liver of blaspheming Jew,
Gall of goat, and slips of yew
Sliver'd in the moon's eclipse;
Nose of Turk, and Tartar's lips;
Finger of birth-strangled babe   30
Ditch-deliver'd by a drab,
Make the gruel thick and slab.
Add thereto a tiger's chawdron,
For th' ingredients of our cawdron.

All. Double, double, toil and trouble;   35
Fire burn, and cauldron bubble.

2 Witch. Cool it with a baboon's blood;
Then the charm is firm and good.

Enter Heccat and the other three Witches.

Heccat. O, well done! I commend your pains,
And every one shall share i' th' gains.   40
And now about the cauldron sing,
Like elves and fairies in a ring,
Enchanting all that you put in.
Music and a song, 'Black Spirits,' etc.
[*Exit Heccat.*]

2 Witch. By the pricking of my thumbs,
Something wicked this way comes.   45
Open, locks, whoever knocks.

23 mummy mummified flesh N. maw and gulf stomach N. 24
ravin'd glutted with prey, or ravenous (?). 31 Ditch-deliver'd
born in a ditch. drab whore. 32 slab thick. 33 chawdron entrails.
34 cawdron cauldron. 37 baboon's stressed ⏑ —. SD Enter
Heccat . . . Witches N. 39–43 O, well done . . . you put in N

Enter Macbeth.

Macbeth. How now, you secret, black, and midnight
 hags?
What is't you do?
 All.   A deed without a name.
 Macbeth. I conjure you, by that which you pro-
 fess—
Howere you come to know it—answer me.   50
Though you untie the winds and let them fight
Against the churches; though the yesty waves
Confound and swallow navigation up;
Though bladed corn be lodg'd and trees blown down;
Though castles topple on their warders' heads; 55
Though palaces and pyramids do slope
Their heads to their foundations; though the treasure
Of nature's germens tumble all together,
Even till destruction sicken; answer me
To what I ask you.
 1 Witch.   Speak.
 2 Witch.   Demand.
 3 Witch.   We'll answer.
 1 Witch. Say if th' hadst rather hear it from our
 mouths,   61
Or from our masters?
 Macbeth.   Call 'em; let me see 'em.
 1 Witch. Pour in sow's blood, that hath eaten
Her nine farrow; grease, that's sweaten
From the murderer's gibbet, throw   65
Into the flame.

---

49 that which you profess i.e. your magic art. 52 yesty frothy.
54 bladed corn grain not yet in the ear. lodg'd beaten flat. 58
germens seeds (see *King Lear*, III.2.8). 64 farrow young pigs.

All. Come, high or low;
Thy self and office deftly show.

Thunder. First Apparition, an Armed Head.

Macbeth. Tell me, thou unknown power—
1 Witch. He
knows thy thought:
Hear his speech, but say thou nought.
1 Apparition. Macbeth! Macbeth! Macbeth! beware Macduff; 70
Beware the Thane of Fife. Dismiss me. Enough.
He descends.

Macbeth. Whate'er thou art, for thy good caution thanks;
Thou hast harp'd my fear aright. But one word more—
1 Witch. He will not be commanded. Here's another,
More potent than the first. 75

Thunder. Second Apparition, a Bloody Child.

2 Apparition. Macbeth! Macbeth! Macbeth!
Macbeth. Had I three ears, I'd hear thee.
2 Apparition. Be bloody, bold, and resolute; laugh to scorn
The power of man; for none of woman born 79
Shall harm Macbeth. *Descends.*

Macbeth. Then live, Macduff; what need I fear of thee?
But yet I'll make assurance double sure,
And take a bond of fate. Thou shalt not live;

---

67 **office** function. SD **First Apparition** N. 73 **harp'd** guessed.
SD **Second Apparition** N. 83 **bond** i.e. further guaranty.

That I may tell pale-hearted fear it lies,
And sleep in spite of thunder.

> *Thunder. Third Apparition, a Child Crowned,*
> *with a tree in his hand.*

What is this, 85
That rises like the issue of a king,
And wears upon his baby brow the round
And top of sovereignty?

All. Listen, but speak not to't.

3 Apparition. Be lion-mettled, proud, and take no
care
Who chafes, who frets, or where conspirers are. 90
Macbeth shall never vanquish'd be until
Great Birnam wood to high Dunsinane hill
Shall come against him. *Descend.*

Macbeth. That will never be:
Who can impress the forest, bid the tree 94
Unfix his earth-bound root? Sweet bodements! good!
Rebellious head, rise never till the wood
Of Birnam rise, and our high-plac'd Macbeth
Shall live the lease of nature, pay his breath
To time and mortal custom. Yet my heart
Throbs to know one thing: tell me, if your art 100
Can tell so much: shall Banquo's issue ever
Reign in this kingdom?

All. Seek to know no more.

Macbeth. I will be satisfied. Deny me this,
And an eternal curse fall on you! Let me know. 104
Why sinks that cauldron? and what noise is this?

Hoboyes.

SD **Third Apparition** N. 92 **Dunsinane** stressed — $\cdot$ — (here
only). SD **Descend** N. 94 **impress** enlist forcibly. 95 **bodements**
prophecies. 96 **head** F *dead* N. 97 **Birnam** F *Byrnan* N. 98 **lease**
of nature normal life-span. 105 **sinks that cauldron** N.

1 Witch. Show!
2 Witch. Show!
3 Witch. Show!
All. Show his eyes, and grieve his heart;
Come like shadows, so depart.   110

*A show of eight Kings and Banquo, [the] last [king]
with a glass in his hand.*

Macbeth. Thou art too like the spirit of Banquo;
    down!
Thy crown does sear mine eyeballs. And thy hair,
Thou other gold-bound brow, is like the first.
A third is like the former. Filthy hags!   114
Why do you show me this?——A fourth? Start, eyes!
What, will the line stretch out to th' crack of doom?
Another yet? A seventh? I'll see no more.
And yet the eighth appears, who bears a glass
Which shows me many more; and some I see
That twofold balls and treble scepters carry.   120
Horrible sight! Now, I see, 'tis true,
For the blood-bolter'd Banquo smiles upon me,
And points at them for his.   [*Apparitions vanish.*]
            What? is this so?

1 Witch. Ay, sir, all this is so. But why
Stands Macbeth thus amazedly?   125
Come, sisters, cheer we up his sprites,
And show the best of our delights.
I'll charm the air to give a sound,
While you perform your antic round,
That this great king may kindly say,   130

SD **A show of eight Kings** N. 116 **crack of doom** sound of the
trumpet on doomsday. 118 **eighth** F *eight.* **glass** N. 120 **twofold**
. . . **scepters** N. 122 **blood-bolter'd** having the hair clotted with
blood. 124–31 **Ay, sir, . . . his welcome pay** N. 129 **antic**
fantastic. **round** dance.

Our duties did his welcome pay.
                    Music. The Witches dance, and vanish.
  Macbeth. Where are they? Gone? Let this perni-
    cious hour
Stand aye accursed in the calendar!
Come in, without there!

                    Enter Lennox.

  Lennox.   What's your grace's will?
  Macbeth. Saw you the weyard sisters?
  Lennox.   No, my lord
  Macbeth. Came they not by you?
  Lennox.   No indeed, my
    lord.   13*s*
  Macbeth. Infected be the air whereon they ride,
And damn'd all those that trust them! I did hear
The galloping of horse. Who was't came by?
  Lennox. 'Tis two or three, my lord, that bring you
    word   140
Macduff is fled to England.
  Macbeth.   Fled to England?
  Lennox. Ay, my good lord.
  Macbeth. Time, thou anticipat'st my dread ex-
    ploits;
The flighty purpose never is o'ertook
Unless the deed go with it. From this moment   145
The very firstlings of my heart shall be
The firstlings of my hand. And even now,
To crown my thoughts with acts, be it thought and
    done:
The castle of Macduff I will surprise,
Seize upon Fife, give to th' edge o' th' sword   150

143 exploit stressed — ´. 144–5 The flighty . . . it N. 146
firstlings first-born.

His wife, his babes, and all unfortunate souls
That trace him in his line. No boasting like a fool;
This deed I'll do before this purpose cool;
But no more sights! Where are these gentlemen?
Come, bring me where they are.   *Exeunt.*

SCENE 2

Enter Macduff's Wife, her Son, and Ross.

Lady Macduff. What had he done to make him fly
   the land?
Ross. You must have patience, madam.
Lady Macduff.   He had
   none.
His flight was madness. When our actions do not,
Our fears do make us traitors.
Ross.   You know not
Whether it was his wisdom or his fear.   5
  Lady Macduff. Wisdom! to leave his wife, to leave
   his babes,
His mansion, and his titles, in a place
From whence himself does fly? He loves us not;
He wants the natural touch. For the poor wren,
The most diminitive of birds, will fight,   10
Her young ones in her nest, against the owl.
All is the fear and nothing is the love;
As little is the wisdom, where the flight
So runs against all reason.
  Ross.   My dearest coz,   14
I pray you school yourself. But, for your husband,

152 **trace** follow, i.e. are related to. 7 **titles** possessions. 9 **wants**
lacks. 10 **diminitive** diminutive. 14 **coz** short for 'cousin.' 15
school control.

He is noble, wise, judicious, and best knows
The fits o' th' season. I dare not speak much further;
But cruel are the times, when we are traitors
And do not know ourselves, when we hold rumor
From what we fear, yet know not what we fear,   20
But float upon a wild and violent sea
Each way, and move. I take my leave of you.
Shall not be long but I'll be here again.
Things at the worst will cease, or else climb upward
To what they were before. My pretty cousin,   25
Blessing upon you!

Lady Macduff. Father'd he is, and yet he's father-
less.

Ross. I am so much a fool, should I stay longer,
It would be my disgrace, and your discomfort: 29
I take my leave at once.   *Exit Ross.*

Lady Macduff.   Sirrah, your father's dead;
And what will you do now? How will you live?

Son. As birds do, mother.

Lady Macduff.   What, with worms and
flies?

Son. With what I get, I mean; and so do they.

Lady Macduff. Poor bird! thou'dst never fear the
net nor lime,
The pit-fall nor the gin.   35

Son. Why should I, mother? Poor birds they are
not set for.
My father is not dead, for all your saying.

Lady Macduff. Yes, he is dead. How wilt thou do
for a father?

Son. Nay, how will you do for a husband?

17 **fits** disorders. 30 **Sirrah** form of address often used by parents
to children. 34 **lime** birdlime. 35 **gin** snare. 36 **they** i.e. traps and
snares.

71

Lady Macduff. Why, I can buy me twenty at any
    market.   40

Son. Then you'll buy 'em to sell again.

Lady Macduff. Thou speak'st with all thy wit;
And yet, i' faith, with wit enough for thee.

Son. Was my father a traitor, mother?

Lady Macduff. Ay, that he was.   45

Son. What is a traitor?

Lady Macduff. Why, one that swears and lies.

Son. And be all traitors that do so?

Lady Macduff. Every one that does so is a traitor,
and must be hang'd.   50

Son. And must they all be hang'd that swear and
lie?

Lady Macduff. Every one.

Son. Who must hang them?

Lady Macduff. Why, the honest men.   55

Son. Then the liars and swearers are fools, for
there are liars and swearers enow to beat the honest
men and hang up them.

Lady Macduff. Now God help thee, poor monkey!
But how wilt thou do for a father?   60

Son. If he were dead, you'd weep for him. If you
would not, it were a good sign that I should quickly
have a new father.

Lady Macduff. Poor prattler, how thou talk'st!

Enter a Messenger.

Messenger. Bless you, fair dame! I am not to you
    known,   65
Though in your state of honor I am perfect.

49–50 **Every one . . . hang'd** F prints as verse. 57 **enow** enough.
59–60 **Now . . . father** F prints as verse. 66 **in . . . perfect** per-
fectly acquainted with your honorable station.

I doubt some danger does approach you nearly.
If you will take a homely man's advice,
Be not found here; hence, with your little ones.
To fright you thus methinks I am too savage;   70
To do worse to you were fell cruelty,
Which is too nigh your person. Heaven preserve
    you!
I dare abide no longer.   *Exit Messenger.*
 Lady Macduff.   Whither should I fly?
I have done no harm. But I remember now
I am in this earthly world, where to do harm   75
Is often laudable, to do good sometime
Accounted dangerous folly. Why then, alas,
Do I put up that womanly defense,
To say I have done no harm?

     Enter Murtherers.

              What are these faces?
Murtherer. Where is your husband?   80
 Lady Macduff. I hope in no place so unsanctified
Where such as thou mayst find him.
 Murtherer.   He's a traitor.
 Son. Thou liest, thou shag-hair'd villain.
 Murtherer.   What!
    you egg.
Young fry of treachery!   [*Stabbing him.*]
 Son.   He has killed me, mother.
Run away, I pray you!   85
    Exit [*Lady Macduff*] *crying 'Murther.'*

67 doubt fear. 68 homely humble. 70 thus methinks F punctuates
thus. *Me thinkes.* 83 shag-hair'd F *shagge-ear'd* N.

SCENE 3

Enter Malcolm and Macduff.

Malcolm. Let us seek out some desolate shade, and there
Weep our sad bosoms empty.
Macduff.   Let us rather
Hold fast the mortal sword, and like good men
Bestride our downfall'n birthdom. Each new morn
New widows howl, new orphans cry, new sorrows   5
Strike heaven on the face, that it resounds
As if it felt with Scotland and yell'd out
Like syllable of dolor.
Malcolm.   What I believe I'll wail,
What know believe, and what I can redress,
As I shall find the time to friend, I will.   10
What you have spoke, it may be so perchance.
This tyrant, whose sole name blisters our tongues,
Was once thought honest; you have lov'd him well;
He hath not touch'd you yet. I am young; but some-
        thing
You may discern of him through me, and wisdom
To offer up a weak, poor, innocent lamb   16
T' appease an angry god.
Macduff. I am not treacherous.
Malcolm.   But Macbeth is.
A good and virtuous nature may recoil   19
In an imperial charge. But I shall crave your pardon

3 **mortal** deadly. 4 **Bestride** i.e. in its defense. **birthdom** father-
land. 10 **to friend** as a friend; i.e. to be favorable. 12 **sole** mere.
15 **discern** learn by discernment N. 19–20 **recoil** . . . **charge** give
way under pressure from a ruler.

That which you are my thoughts cannot transpose;
Angels are bright still, though the brightest fell.
Though all things foul would wear the brows of
    grace,
Yet grace must still look so.
  Macduff.   I have lost my hopes.
  Malcolm. Perchance even there where I did find my
    doubts.   25
Why in that rawness left you wife and child,
Those precious motives, those strong knots of love,
Without leave-taking? I pray you,
Let not my jealousies be your dishonors,
But mine own safeties. You may be rightly just,   30
Whatever I shall think.
  Macduff.   Bleed, bleed, poor country!
Great tyranny, lay thou thy basis sure,
For goodness dare not check thee! Wear thou thy
    wrongs;
The title is affeer'd! Fare thee well, lord.
I would not be the villain that thou think'st   35
For the whole space that's in the tyrant's grasp,
And the rich East to boot.
  Malcolm.   Be not offended.
I speak not as in absolute fear of you.
I think our country sinks beneath the yoke;
It weeps, it bleeds, and each new day a gash   40
Is added to her wounds. I think withal,
There would be hands uplifted in my right;
And here from gracious England have I offer

---

21 transpose alter. 24 so i.e. like itself. 26 rawness unprotected
condition. 27 motives persons inspiring love and action. 29 jealousies suspicions. 34 affeer'd confirmed; F *affear'd*. 43 gracious
England i.e. the English king, Edward the Confessor.

Of goodly thousands. But, for all this,
When I shall tread upon the tyrant's head,   45
Or wear it on my sword, yet my poor country
Shall have more vices than it had before,
More suffer, and more sundry ways than ever,
By him that shall succeed.
   Macduff.   What should he be?
   Malcolm. It is myself I mean; in whom I know   50
All the particulars of vice so grafted
That, when they shall be open'd, black Macbeth
Will seem as pure as snow, and the poor state
Esteem him as a lamb, being compar'd
With my confineless harms.
   Macduff.   Not in the legions   55
Of horrid hell can come a divel more damn'd
In evils to top Macbeth.
   Malcolm.   I grant him bloody,
Luxurious, avaricious, false, deceitful,
Sudden, malicious, smacking of every sin
That has a name. But there's no bottom, none,   60
In my voluptuousness: your wives, your daughters,
Your matrons, and your maids, could not fill up
The cistern of my lust, and my desire
All continent impediments would o'erbear
That did oppose my will. Better Macbeth   65
Than such an one to reign.
   Macduff.   Boundless intemperance
In nature is a tyranny. It hath been
Th' untimely emptying of the happy throne,
And fall of many kings. But fear not yet
To take upon you what is yours; you may   70
Convey your pleasures in a spacious plenty,

55 **confineless** boundless. 58 **Luxurious** lustful. 64 **continent** restraining. 71 **Convey** arrange secretly.

And yet seem cold, the time you may so hoodwink.
We have willing dames enough; there cannot be
That vulture in you, to devour so many
As will to greatness dedicate themselves,   75
Finding it so inclin'd.
   Malcolm.   With this there grows
In my most ill-compos'd affection such
A stanchless avarice that, were I king,
I should cut off the nobles for their lands,
Desire his jewels and this other's house;   80
And my more-having would be as a sauce
To make me hunger more, that I should forge
Quarrels unjust against the good and loyal,
Destroying them for wealth.
   Macduff.   This avarice
Sticks deeper, grows with more pernicious root   85
Than summer-seeming lust, and it hath been
The sword of our slain kings. Yet do not fear;
Scotland hath foisons to fill up your will
Of your mere own. All these are portable,
With other graces weigh'd.   90
   Malcolm. But I have none. The king-becoming
      graces,
As justice, verity, temp'rance, stableness,
Bounty, perseverance, mercy, lowliness,
Devotion, patience, courage, fortitude,
I have no relish of them, but abound   95

---

72 **cold, the time** F punctuates *cold. The time.* **time** see I.5.64 N.
77 **affection** disposition. 78 **stanchless** insatiable. 86 **summer-
seeming** befitting (beseeming) summer, or resembling it. 87 **sword**
i.e. cause of death. 88 **foisons** plentiful supplies. 89 **your mere own**
what is entirely yours. **portable** endurable. 90 **With . . . weigh'd**
i.e. when balanced against other graces. 93 **perseverance** read
'persév'rance.'

In the division of each several crime,
Acting it many ways. Nay, had I power, I should
Pour the sweet milk of concord into hell,
Uproar the universal peace, confound
All unity on earth.
   Macduff.   O Scotland, Scotland!   100
   Malcolm. If such a one be fit to govern, speak.
I am as I have spoken.
   Macduff.   Fit to govern?
No, not to live. O nation miserable!
With an untitled tyrant bloody-scept'red,
When shalt thou see thy wholesome days again,   105
Since that the truest issue of thy throne
By his own interdiction stands accus'd,
And does blaspheme his breed? Thy royal father
Was a most sainted king; the queen that bore thee,
Oft'ner upon her knees than on her feet,   110
Died every day she liv'd. Fare thee well!
These evils thou repeat'st upon thyself
Hath banish'd me from Scotland. O my breast,
Thy hope ends here!
   Malcolm.   Macduff, this noble passion,
Child of integrity, hath from my soul   115
Wip'd the black scruples, reconcil'd my thoughts
To thy good truth and honor. Divelish Macbeth
By many of these trains hath sought to win me
Into his power, and modest wisdom plucks me
From overcredulous haste; but God above   120
Deal between thee and me! for even now
I put myself to thy direction, and

---

96 division variation. 98–100 Pour . . . earth N. 107 interdiction
statement of unfitness (legal term). 111 Died . . . liv'd i.e. was
always ready for death; see I Corinthians 15:31. 113 Hath have.
118 trains stratagems. 119 modest marked by moderation.

Unspeak mine own detraction, here abjure
The taints and blames I laid upon myself,
For strangers to my nature. I am yet   125
Unknown to woman, never was forsworn,
Scarcely have coveted what was mine own,
At no time broke my faith, would not betray
The devil to his fellow, and delight   129
No less in truth than life. My first false speaking
Was this upon myself. What I am truly
Is thine and my poor country's to command;
Whither indeed, before thy here-approach,
Old Siward, with ten thousand warlike men,
Already at a point, was setting forth.   135
Now we'll together, and the chance of goodness
Be like our warranted quarrel. Why are you silent?
  Macduff. Such welcome and unwelcome things at
        once
'Tis hard to reconcile.

Enter a Doctor.

Malcolm. Well, more anon. Comes the king forth,
        I pray you?   140
  Doctor. Ay, sir; there are a crew of wretched souls
That stay his cure; their malady convinces
The great assay of art. But, at his touch,
Such sanctity hath heaven given his hand,
They presently amend.
  Malcolm.   I thank you, doctor.   145
                    Exit [*Doctor.*]

125 For as being. 133 thy F *they*. 135 at a point in readiness.
136–7 the chance . . . quarrel N. 142 stay his cure wait for him
to cure them N. 142–3 convinces . . . art conquers the greatest
efforts of medical skill. 145 presently immediately.

Macduff. What's the disease he means?
Malcolm.   'Tis call'd
    the evil.
A most miraculous work in this good king,
Which often, since my here-remain in England,
I have seen him do. How he solicits heaven,   149
Himself best knows; but strangely-visited people,
All swolne and ulcerous, pitiful to the eye,
The mere despair of surgery, he cures,
Hanging a golden stamp about their necks,
Put on with holy prayers; and 'tis spoken
To the succeeding royalty he leaves   155
The healing benediction. With this strange virtue,
He hath a heavenly gift of prophecy,
And sundry blessings hang about his throne
That speak him full of grace.

Enter Ross.

Macduff.   See who comes here.
Malcolm. My countryman; but yet I know him not.
Macduff. My ever-gentle cousin, welcome hither.
Malcolm. I know him now. Good God, betimes remove
The means that makes us strangers!
Ross.   Sir, amen.
Macduff. Stands Scotland where it did?
Ross.   Alas, poor
    country,
Almost afraid to know itself! It cannot   165
Be call'd our mother, but our grave; where nothing,
But who knows nothing, is once seen to smile;

146 evil see IV.3.142 N. 150 visited afflicted. 151 swolne swollen.
152 mere utter. 153 **stamp** stamped coin. 161 gentle noble. 162
betimes speedily.

Where sighs and groans and shrieks that rent the air
Are made, not mark'd; where violent sorrow seems
A modern ecstasy; the dead man's knell   170
Is there scarce ask'd for who; and good men's lives
Expire before the flowers in their caps,
Dying or ere they sicken.

  Macduff.   O, relation
Too nice, and yet too true.

  Malcolm.   What's the newest grief?

  Ross. That of an hour's age doth hiss the speaker;
Each minute teems a new one.

  Macduff.   How does my wife?

  Ross. Why, well.

  Macduff.   And all my children?

  Ross.   Well too.

  Macduff. The tyrant has not batter'd at their
    peace?

  Ross. No; they were well at peace when I did leave
'em.

  Macduff. Be not a niggard of your speech: how
    goes't?   180

  Ross. When I came hither to transport the tidings
Which I have heavily borne, there ran a rumor
Of many worthy fellows that were out;
Which was to my belief witness'd the rather
For that I saw the tyrant's power afoot.   185
Now is the time of help; your eye in Scotland
Would create soldiers, make our women fight,
To doff their dire distresses.

  Malcolm.   Be't their comfort

---

170 ecstasy frenzy N. 173 or ere ere. relation recital. 174 nice
minutely accurate. 175 hiss cause to be hissed for giving out-
dated information. 176 teems gives birth to. 183 out i.e. in the
field in arms. 185 power army.

We are coming thither. Gracious England hath
Lent us good Siward and ten thousand men;　190
An older and a better soldier none
That Christendom gives out.
　　Ross.　　　　　　　　Would I could answer
This comfort with the like! But I have words
That would be howl'd out in the desert air,
Where hearing them should not latch them.
　　Macduff.　　　　　　　　What
　　　concern they?　195
The general cause? or is it a fee-grief
Due to some single breast?
　　Ross.　　　　　　　No mind that's honest
But in it shares some woe, though the main part
Pertains to you alone.
　　Macduff.　　　　If it be mine,
Keep it not from me; quickly let me have it.　200
　　Ross. Let not your ears despise my tongue forever,
Which shall possess them with the heaviest sound
That ever yet they heard.
　　Macduff.　　　　Humh! I guess at it.
　　Ross. Your castle is surpris'd; your wife and babes
Savagely slaughter'd. To relate the manner　205
Were, on the quarry of these murther'd deer,
To add the death of you.
　　Malcolm.　　　　Merciful heaven!
What, man! Ne'er pull your hat upon your brows.
Give sorrow words; the grief that does not speak
Whispers the o'er-fraught heart and bids it break.
　　Macduff. My children too?　211

189 **Gracious England** see l. 43. 192 **gives out** proclaims. 194
would be demand to be. 195 **latch** catch. 196 **fee-grief** private
grief. 202 **heaviest** most grievous. 206 **quarry** game killed in
hunting.

Ross. Wife, children, servants, all that could be
found.

Macduff. And I must be from thence! My wife kill'd
too?

Ross. I have said.

Malcolm.   Be comforted.
Let's make us med'cines of our great revenge,   215
To cure this deadly grief.

Macduff. He has no children. All my pretty ones?
Did you say all? O hell-kite! All?
What, all my pretty chickens and their dam
At one fell swoop?   220

Malcolm. Dispute it like a man.

Macduff.   I shall do so;
But I must also feel it as a man.
I cannot but remember such things were,
That were most precious to me. Did heaven look on,
And would not take their part? Sinful Macduff,
They were all struck for thee! Naught that I am,
Not for their own demerits, but for mine,
Fell slaughter on their souls. Heaven rest them now!

Malcolm. Be this the whetstone of your sword; let
grief   229
Convert to anger; blunt not the heart, enrage it.

Macduff. O, I could play the woman with mine eyes,
And braggart with my tongue. But, gentle heavens,
Cut short all intermission. Front to front
Bring thou this fiend of Scotland and myself;
Within my sword's length set him; if he scape,   235
Heaven forgive him too!

Malcolm.   This tune goes manly.

220 **swoop** i.e. of the hell-kite. 221 **dispute it** contest it (Macbeth's
action); i.e. avenge yourself N. 226 **Naught** wicked man. 233 **intermission** delay. 236 **tune** F *time.*

Come, go we to the king; our power is ready;
Our lack is nothing but our leave. Macbeth
Is ripe for shaking, and the powers above
Put on their instruments. Receive what cheer you
    may;   240
The night is long that never finds the day. *Exeunt.*

237 power army. 238 Our lack . . . leave we need only permission to go. 240 Put on their instruments arm themselves.

Act V

SCENE 1

*Enter a Doctor of Physic and
a Waiting Gentlewoman.*

Doctor. I have two nights watch'd with you, but
can perceive no truth in your report. When was it
she last walk'd?   3

Gentlewoman. Since his majesty went into the field,
I have seen her rise from her bed, throw her night-
gown upon her, unlock her closet, take forth paper,
fold it, write upon't, read it, afterwards seal it, and
again return to bed; yet all this while in a most fast
sleep.   9

Doctor. A great perturbation in nature, to receive
at once the benefit of sleep and do the effects of
watching! In this slumb'ry agitation, besides her
walking and other actual performances, what, at any
time, have you heard her say?   14

Gentlewoman. That, sir, which I will not report
after her.

Doctor. You may to me, and 'tis most meet you
should.

Gentlewoman. Neither to you nor anyone, having
no witness to confirm my speech.   20

4 into the field i.e. to battle. 5–6 night-gown dressing gown.
6 closet private repository of valuables. 11–12 effects of watching
actions of a waking condition.

Enter Lady, with a taper.

Lo you, here she comes. This is her very guise, and upon my life, fast asleep. Observe her; stand close.

Doctor. How came she by that light?

Gentlewoman. Why, it stood by her. She has light by her continually; 'tis her command. 25

Doctor. You see her eyes are open.

Gentlewoman. Ay, but their sense are shut.

Doctor. What is it she does now? Look how she rubs her hands. 29

Gentlewoman. It is an accustom'd action with her, to seem thus washing her hands. I have known her continue in this a quarter of an hour.

Lady Macbeth. Yet here's a spot.

Doctor. Hark! she speaks. I will set down what comes from her, to satisfy my remembrance the more strongly. 36

Lady Macbeth. Out, damned spot! out, I say! One; two. Why, then, 'tis time to do't. Hell is murky. Fie, my lord, fie! a soldier, and afeard? What need we fear who knows it, when none can call our power to accompt? Yet who would have thought the old man to have had so much blood in him? 42

Doctor. Do you mark that?

Lady Macbeth. The Thane of Fife had a wife. Where is she now? What, will these hands ne'er be clean? No more o' that, my lord, no more o' that! You mar all with this starting. 47

Doctor. Go to, go to! You have known what you should not.

Gentlewoman. She has spoke what she should not, I am sure of that. Heaven knows what she has known.

Lady Macbeth. Here's the smell of the blood still. All the perfumes of Arabia will not sweeten this little hand. Oh, oh, oh!   54

Doctor. What a sigh is there! The heart is sorely charg'd.

Gentlewoman. I would not have such a heart in my bosom for the dignity of the whole body.

Doctor. Well, well, well.

Gentlewoman. Pray God it be, sir.   60

Doctor. This disease is beyond my practice. Yet I have known those which have walk'd in their sleep who have died holily in their beds.

Lady Macbeth. Wash your hands, put on your night-gown, look not so pale. I tell you yet again, Banquo's buried; he cannot come out on's grave.

Doctor. Even so?   67

Lady Macbeth. To bed, to bed! There's knocking at the gate. Come, come, come, come, give me your hand. What's done cannot be undone. To bed, to bed, to bed!   *Exit Lady.*

Doctor. Will she go now to bed?   72

Gentlewoman. Directly.

Doctor. Foul whisp'rings are abroad. Unnatural deeds

Do breed unnatural troubles. Infected minds   75
To their deaf pillows will discharge their secrets.
More needs she the divine than the physician.
God, God forgive us all! Look after her;
Remove from her the means of all annoyance,
And still keep eyes upon her. So, good night.   80

55–6 **sorely charg'd** heavily burdened. 58 **dignity** worth. 66 **on's** of his. 79 **annoyance** injury (to herself).

My mind she has mated, and amaz'd my sight.
I think, but dare not speak.
    Gentlewoman.   Good night, good doctor.
                                   Exeunt.

SCENE 2

Drum and colors. Enter Menteth, Cathness, Angus,
Lennox, Soldiers.

   Menteth. The English power is near, led on by
    Malcolm,
His uncle Siward, and the good Macduff.
Revenges burn in them; for their dear causes
Would to the bleeding and the grim alarm
Excite the mortified man.
   Angus.   Near Birnam wood   5
Shall we well meet them; that way are they coming.
   Cathness. Who knows if Donalbain be with his
    brother?
   Lennox. For certain, sir, he is not. I have a file
Of all the gentry: there is Siward's son,
And many unrough youths that even now   10
Protest their first of manhood.
   Menteth.   What does the
    tyrant?
   Cathness. Great Dunsinane he strongly fortifies.
Some say he's mad; others that lesser hate him
Do call it valiant fury; but, for certain,
He cannot buckle his distemper'd cause   15

81 **mated** bewildered. 1 **power** army. 3 **dear** heartfelt. 4 **alarm** call
to battle. 5 **mortified** numbed, or even dead. 10 **unrough** un-
bearded. 11 **Protest** proclaim. 15 **distemper'd** sick, unruly.
   88

Within the belt of rule.

   Angus.   Now does he feel
His secret murthers sticking on his hands;
Now minutely revolts upbraid his faith-breach.
Those he commands move only in command,
Nothing in love. Now does he feel his title   20
Hang loose about him, like a giant's robe
Upon a dwarfish thief.

   Menteth.   Who then shall blame
His pester'd senses to recoil and start,
When all that is within him does condemn
Itself for being there?

   Cathness.   Well, march we on,   25
To give obedience where 'tis truly ow'd.
Meet we the med'cine of the sickly weal,
And with him pour we in our country's purge
Each drop of us.

   Lennox.   Or so much as it needs   29
To dew the sovereign flower and drown the weeds.
Make we our march towards Birnam.

                              Exeunt marching.

SCENE 3

Enter Macbeth, Doctor, and Attendants.

   Macbeth. Bring me no more reports; let them fly
all!
Till Birnam wood remove to Dunsinane
I cannot taint with fear. What's the boy Malcolm?

18 minutely (stressed $-' - -$) happening every minute. 20
Nothing not at all. 23 pester'd troubled. 27 med'cine physician.
weal state. 30 dew literally 'water,' figuratively 'make grow.'
sovereign flower N. 3 taint become tainted.

Was he not born of woman? The spirits that know
All mortal consequences have pronounc'd me thus:
'Fear not, Macbeth; no man that's born of woman
Shall ere have power upon thee.' Then fly, false
 thanes,
And mingle with the English epicures!
The mind I sway by and the heart I bear   9
Shall never sag with doubt nor shake with fear.

Enter Servant.

The divel damn thee black, thou cream-fac'd loon!
Where got'st thou that goose look?
 Servant. There is ten thousand—
 Macbeth.   Geese, villain?
 Servant.   Soldiers, sir.
 Macbeth. Go prick thy face, and over-red thy fear,
Thou lily-liver'd boy. What soldiers, patch? 15
Death of thy soul! those linen cheeks of thine
Are counselors to fear. What soldiers, wheyface?
 Servant. The English force, so please you.
 Macbeth. Take thy face hence. [*Exit Servant.*]
          Seyton!—I am sick
 at heart
When I behold—Seyton, I say!—This push 20
Will cheer me ever or disseat me now.
I have liv'd long enough. My way of life
Is falne into the sear, the yellow leaf;
And that which should accompany old age,
As honor, love, obedience, troops of friends, 25

5 **mortal consequences** future events in human life. 9 **sway** control myself. 11 **cream-fac'd** the servant's face is white with fear. **loon** rascal, lout. 14 **over-red** cover with red. 15 **patch** clown, fool. 20 **push** crisis, attack. 21 **cheer** N. **disseat** unseat; F *dis-eate.* 23 **falne** fallen.

90

I must not look to have; but, in their steed,
Curses, not loud but deep, mouth-honor, breath,
Which the poor heart would fain deny, and dare not.
Seyton!

Enter Seyton.

Seyton. What's your gracious pleasure?
Macbeth. What
news more? 30
Seyton. All is confirm'd, my lord, which was re-
ported.
Macbeth. I'll fight till from my bones my flesh be
hack'd.
Give me my armor.
Seyton. 'Tis not needed yet.
Macbeth. I'll put it on.
Send out moe horses, skirr the country round; 35
Hang those that talk of fear. Give me mine armor.
How does your patient, doctor?
Doctor. Not so sick, my lord,
As she is troubled with thick-coming fancies
That keep her from her rest.
Macbeth. Cure her of that!
Canst thou not minister to a mind diseas'd, 40
Pluck from the memory a rooted sorrow,
Raze out the written troubles of the brain,
And with some sweet oblivious antidote
Cleanse the stuff'd bosom of that perilous stuff
Which weighs upon the heart?
Doctor. Therein the patient
Must minister to himself. 46

26 steed stead. 35 moe more. **skirr** scour. 39 her F omits. 42 **Raze
out** erase. **written** i.e. permanent. 43 **oblivious** causing forgetful-
ness.

Macbeth. Throw physic to the dogs; I'll none of it.
Come, put mine armor on. Give me my staff.
Seyton, send out.—Doctor, the thanes fly from me.—
Come, sir, dispatch.—If thou couldst, doctor, cast
The water of my land, find her disease,   51
And purge it to a sound and pristine health,
I would applaud thee to the very echo,
That should applaud again.—Pull't off, I say.—
What rhubarb, cyme, or what purgative drug   55
Would scour these English hence? Hear'st thou of
      them?

Doctor. Ay, my good lord. Your royal preparation
Makes us hear something.

Macbeth.   Bring it after me.
I will not be afraid of death and bane
Till Birnam forest come to Dunsinane.   60

Doctor. [*Aside.*] Were I from Dunsinane away and
      clear,
Profit again should hardly draw me here.   *Exeunt.*

SCENE 4

Drum and colors. Enter Malcolm, Siward, Macduff,
Siward's Son, Menteth, Cathness, Angus, [Lennox,
Ross,] and Soldiers marching.

Malcolm. Cousins, I hope the days are near at hand
That chambers will be safe.

Menteth.   We doubt it nothing.

Siward. What wood is this before us?

Menteth.   The wood of
      Birnam.

50–1 cast/The water analyze the urine. 55 cyme a cathartic N.
2 chambers will be safe i.e. we can sleep in security.

Malcolm. Let every soldier hew him down a bough
And bear't before him: thereby shall we shadow 5
The numbers of our host, and make discovery
Err in report of us.

Soldier.   It shall be done.

Siward. We learn no other but the confident tyrant
Keeps still in Dunsinane, and will endure
Our setting down before't.

Malcolm.   'Tis his main hope; 10
For where there is advantage to be given,
Both more and less have given him the revolt,
And none serve with him but constrained things
Whose hearts are absent too.

Macduff.   Let our just censures
Attend the true event, and put we on 15
Industrious soldiership.

Siward.   The time approaches
That will with due decision make us know
What we shall say we have and what we owe.
Thoughts speculative their unsure hopes relate,
But certain issue strokes must arbitrate, 20
Towards which advance the war.   *Exeunt marching.*

5 **shadow** partially conceal. 6 **discovery** reconnaissance. 10 **setting down before** laying siege to. 11 **where . . . given** i.e. where opportunity is offered. 12 **more and less** high and low. 14–15 **Let . . . event** Let's wait until after the battle to make a true judgment. 14 **censures** judgments. 15 **event** outcome. 18 **owe** own (in fact, as opposed to what we 'say we have'). 19–20 **Thoughts . . . arbitrate** N.

SCENE 5

*Enter Macbeth, Seyton, and Soldiers,
with drum and colors.*

Macbeth. Hang out our banners on the outward
walls.
The cry is still, 'They come.' Our castle's strength
Will laugh a siege to scorn. Here let them lie
Till famine and the ague eat them up.   4
Were they not forc'd with those that should be ours,
We might have met them dareful, beard to beard,
And beat them backward home.

                              A cry within of women.
                                    What is that noise?
Seyton. It is the cry of women, my good lord.
                                                [Exit.]
Macbeth. I have almost forgot the taste of fears.
The time has been, my senses would have cool'd   10
To hear a night-shriek, and my fell of hair
Would at a dismal treatise rouse and stir
As life were in't. I have supp'd full with horrors;
Direness, familiar to my slaughterous thoughts,
Cannot once start me.

[Enter Seyton.]

                    Wherefore was that cry?   15
Seyton. The queen, my lord, is dead.
Macbeth. She should have died hereafter;
There would have been a time for such a word.

5 **forc'd** reinforced. 11 **fell of hair** skin with hair growing on it.
12 **treatise** story. 15 **start** startle. 17 **should** would. 18 **word** i.e.
the announcement of her death.

Tomorrow, and tomorrow, and tomorrow,
Creeps in this petty pace from day to day,   20
To the last syllable of recorded time;
And all our yesterdays have lighted fools
The way to dusty death. Out, out, brief candle!
Life's but a walking shadow, a poor player
That struts and frets his hour upon the stage,   25
And then is heard no more. It is a tale
Told by an idiot, full of sound and fury,
Signifying nothing.

Enter a Messenger.

Thou com'st to use thy tongue; thy story quickly.
  Messenger. Gracious my lord,   30
I should report that which I say I saw,
But know not how to do't.
  Macbeth.   Well, say, sir.
  Messenger. As I did stand my watch upon the hill,
I look'd toward Birnam, and anon, methought,
The wood began to move.
  Macbeth.   Liar and slave!   35
  Messenger. Let me endure your wrath if't be not so:
Within this three mile may you see it coming;
I say, a moving grove.
  Macbeth.   If thou speak'st false,
Upon the next tree shall thou hang alive
Till famine cling thee. If thy speech be sooth,   40
I care not if thou dost for me as much.
I pull in resolution and begin
To doubt th' equivocation of the fiend
That lies like truth. 'Fear not, till Birnam wood

24–5 **Life's . . . stage** see II.4.6 N. 39 **shall** shalt. 40 **cling** wither.
sooth truth. 42 **pull in** rein in. **resolution** assurance, confidence.
95

Do come to Dunsinane,' and now a wood   45
Comes toward Dunsinane. Arm, arm, and out!
If this which he avouches does appear,
There is nor flying hence, nor tarrying here.
I gin to be aweary of the sun,
And wish th' estate o' th' world were now undone.
Ring the alarum bell! Blow, wind! come, wrack!   51
At least we'll die with harness on our back. *Exeunt.*

SCENE 6

*Drum and colors. Enter Malcolm, Siward, Macduff,
and their Army, with boughs.*

Malcolm. Now near enough; your leavy screens
    throw down,
And show like those you are. You, worthy uncle,
Shall with my cousin, your right-noble son,
Lead our first battle. Worthy Macduff and we
Shall take upon's what else remains to do,   5
According to our order.
Siward.   Fare you well.
Do we but find the tyrant's power tonight,
Let us be beaten, if we cannot fight.
Macduff. Make all our trumpets speak; give them
    all breath,
Those clamorous harbingers of blood and death.   10
               Exeunt. Alarums continued.

50 **estate o' th' world** orderly universe. 51 **wrack** ruin. 1 **leavy**
leafy. 4 **battle** part of the army.

SCENE 7

Enter Macbeth.

Macbeth. They have tied me to a stake; I cannot
fly,
But bearlike I must fight the course. What's he
That was not born of woman? Such a one
Am I to fear, or none.

Enter Young Siward.

Young Siward. What is thy name?
Macbeth.   Thou'lt be
afraid to hear it.   5
Young Siward. No; though thou call'st thyself a
hotter name
Than any is in hell.
Macbeth.   My name's Macbeth.
Young Siward. The divel himself could not pro-
nounce a title
More hateful to mine ear.
Macbeth.   No, nor more fearful.
Young Siward. Thou liest, abhorred tyrant; with
my sword   10
I'll prove the lie thou speak'st.
               Fight, and Young Siward slain.
Macbeth.   Thou wast born of
woman;
But swords I smile at, weapons laugh to scorn,
Brandish'd by man that's of a woman born.   *Exit.*

2 bearlike . . . course N. SD Exit N.

Alarums. Enter Macduff.

Macduff. That way the noise is. Tyrant, show thy
face!

If thou be'st slain and with no stroke of mine,   15
My wife and children's ghosts will haunt me still.
I cannot strike at wretched kerns, whose arms
Are hir'd to bear their staves; either thou, Macbeth,
Or else my sword with an unbatter'd edge
I sheathe again undeeded. There thou shouldst be.
By this great clatter, one of greatest note   21
Seems bruited. Let me find him, fortune!
And more I beg not.   *Exit. Alarums.*

Enter Malcolm and Siward.

Siward. This way, my lord; the castle's gently
rend'red;

The tyrant's people on both sides do fight;   25
The noble thanes do bravely in the war;
The day almost itself professes yours,
And little is to do.

Malcolm.   We have met with foes
That strike beside us.

Siward.   Enter, sir, the castle.

                        Exeunt. Alarum.

Enter Macbeth.

Macbeth. Why should I play the Roman fool, and
die   30

17 **kerns** see I.2.13. 18 **staves** spears. 22 **bruited** noised, reported.
24 **rend'red** surrendered. 26 **bravely** worthily, excellently. 29
strike beside us deliberately miss us. SD **Enter Macbeth** N.
30 **Roman fool** i.e. Brutus, Antony, etc.

On mine own sword? whiles I see lives, the gashes
Do better upon them.

Enter Macduff.

Macduff.   Turn, hell-hound, turn!
Macbeth. Of all men else I have avoided thee.
But get thee back, my soul is too much charg'd
With blood of thine already.
Macduff.   I have no words;   35
My voice is in my sword, thou bloodier villain
Than terms can give thee out!   *Fight. Alarum.*
Macbeth.   Thou losest labor.
As easy mayst thou the intrenchant air
With thy keen sword impress, as make me bleed.
Let fall thy blade on vulnerable crests;   40
I bear a charmed life, which must not yield
To one of woman born.
Macduff.   Despair thy charm;
And let the angel whom thou still hast serv'd
Tell thee, Macduff was from his mother's womb
Untimely ripp'd.   45
Macbeth. Accursed be that tongue that tells me so,
For it hath cow'd my better part of man!
And be these juggling fiends no more believ'd,
That palter with us in a double sense;
That keep the word of promise to our ear,   50
And break it to our hope. I'll not fight with thee.
Macduff. Then yield thee, coward,
And live to be the show and gaze o' th' time.
We'll have thee, as our rarer monsters are,

31 lives i.e. living enemies. 38 **intrenchant** incapable of being cut.
43 **still** always. 47 **better part of man** i.e. valor. 49 **palter** equivocate.

99

Painted upon a pole, and underwrit,   55
'Here may you see the tyrant.'

Macbeth.   I will not yield,
To kiss the ground before young Malcolm's feet,
And to be baited with the rabble's curse.
Though Birnam wood be come to Dunsinane,
And thou oppos'd, being of no woman born,   60
Yet I will try the last. Before my body
I throw my warlike shield. Lay on, Macduff,
And damn'd be him that first cries, 'Hold, enough!'
                    Exeunt fighting. Alarums.

Enter fighting, and Macbeth slain.

Retreat and flourish. Enter, with drum and colors,
Malcolm, Siward, Ross, Thanes, and Soldiers.

Malcolm. I would the friends we miss were safe
          arriv'd.   64
Siward. Some must go off; and yet, by these I see,
So great a day as this is cheaply bought.
Malcolm. Macduff is missing, and your noble son.
Ross. Your son, my lord, has paid a soldier's debt.
He only liv'd but till he was a man,
The which no sooner had his prowess confirm'd   70
In the unshrinking station where he fought,
But like a man he died.
Siward.   Then he is dead?
Ross. Ay, and brought off the field. Your cause of
          sorrow
Must not be measur'd by his worth, for then
It hath no end.

55 **Painted upon a pole** i.e. with a painted likeness suspended on a
pole. 58 **baited** i.e. like a bear; see V.7.2 N. SD **Retreat** trumpet
signal to cease pursuit. 65 **go off** stage metaphor for 'die.' 71 **un-**
shrinking station i.e. the station where he did not shrink

Siward.   Had he his hurts before?   75
Ross. Ay, on the front.
Siward.   Why then, God's soldier **be**
he!
Had I as many sons as I have hairs,
I would not wish them to a fairer death;
And so, his knell is knoll'd.
   Malcolm.   He's worth more sorrow,
And that I'll spend for him.
   Siward.   He's worth no more;   80
They say he parted well, and paid his score,
And so, God be with him! Here comes newer comfort.

Enter Macduff, with Macbeth's head.

Macduff. Hail, king! for so thou art. Behold, where
stands
Th' usurper's cursed head; the time is free.
I see thee compass'd with thy kingdom's pearl,   85
That speak my salutation in their minds;
Whose voices I desire aloud with mine;
Hail, King of Scotland!
   All.   Hail, King of Scotland!
                        Flourish.

Malcolm. We shall not spend a large expense of
time
Before we reckon with your several loves,   90
And make us even with you. My thanes and kinsmen,
Henceforth be earls, the first that ever Scotland
In such an honor nam'd. What's more to do,
Which would be planted newly with the time—
As calling home our exil'd friends abroad   95

---

77 **hairs** pronounced like 'heirs.' 81 **score** account. 85 **pearl** i.e. the
nobles. 90 **several loves** devotion of each of you.

That fled the snares of watchful tyranny,
Producing forth the cruel ministers
Of this dead butcher and his fiendlike queen,
Who, as 'tis thought, by self and violent hands
Took off her life—this, and what needful else   100
That calls upon us, by the grace of Grace
We will perform in measure, time, and place.
So, thanks to all at once and to each one,
Whom we invite to see us crown'd at Scone.

Flourish. Exeunt omnes.

FINIS

99 self and violent her own violent. 102 in measure in proportion, with proper decorum.

NOTES

Act I, Scene 1

SD **Thunder and lightning** The scenes with the witches were probably staged in a spectacular fashion. The witches may have been revealed on the inner stage by drawing back a curtain; each of their appearances is accompanied by stage thunder, which was produced by beating drums or by rolling a heavy ball of iron or stone down an uneven set of steps constructed in the superstructure over the stage. The lightning was made by blowing rosin through a candle flame. A stage mist, made by burning rosin, may have risen through the trap door to make the witches disappear in the 'fog and filthy air' at the end of this scene, as also at I.3.78.

8–12 **Graymalkin . . . air** The witches answer the calls of their 'familiars' or attendant spirits, which have assumed the forms of animals. *Graymalkin* is a pet name for a grey cat; *Paddock* means 'toad.' The familiar of the Third Witch, unnamed here, is called *Harpier* in IV.1.3, possibly a corruption of 'harpy.' F ascribes the lines "Paddock calls . . . filthy air" to *All;* the arrangement adopted here is clearly more logical.

Act I, Scene 2

3 **sergeant** A title which a commissioned officer might have in the army of Shakespeare's time. Modern editors often unnecessarily change *Captain* to *Sergeant* in the stage directions and speech headings.

21 **Which** Probably refers to Macdonwald, who never took leave of Macbeth until Macbeth killed him. It may refer to Macbeth; it is possible that the omission of some lines has obscured the sense. A touch of grim humor is added by reference to polite forms of leave-taking: 'shook hands,' 'bade farewell.'

25–6 **As whence . . . thunders break** Storms come out of the east, whence the sun rises.

41 **memorize another Golgotha** Make the field memorable as another 'place of the skull,' the literal meaning of Golgotha, where Christ was crucified.

46 **Thane** A title of nobility in Scotland, corresponding to the English earl.

51–2 flout . . . cold Insult the Scottish sky and chill the people with fear.

58 rebellious Sweno, though not a rebel, was assisting rebellion.

65 general Here and in many other words such as *prosperous*, *treasonous*, *interim*, etc. a lightly accented syllable following a heavily accented syllable may be omitted in pronunciation. Note also that phrases such as 'to the' and 'to his' may be pronounced 'to th' ' and 'to's.'

66–7 deceive . . . interest Betray the interests closest to our heart. Here as elsewhere the king uses the royal plural.

Act I, Scene 3

15 ports they blow The meaning seems to be that she will delay the *Tiger's* arrival in port.

20 penthouse lid The eyelid is compared to a penthouse, that is, a lean-to.

32 weyard One form of 'weird,' derived from the Old English *wyrd*, 'fate.' F uses the forms *weyard* and *weyward* (possibly by association with 'wayward'), but never 'weird,' which has become familiar because of Theobald's 18th-century emendation. The form *weyard* preserves the original meter. The exact nature of the 'weyard sisters' is left undefined: they are not merely old hags practicing sorcery, nor are they truly fates, as they appear to be in Holinshed's *Chronicle*, one of the chief sources of the play (see Appendix B).

35 thrice to thine . . . to make up nine The witches probably make obeisances to their familiars.

46 beards A beard on a woman was often thought to indicate that she was a witch.

93–4 His wonders . . . Silenc'd with that Since the king is unable to decide whether astonishment or admiration better answers Macbeth's accomplishment, or better expresses his own feeling, he is reduced to silence.

143–6 Shakes . . . rapt Here and in a number of other places (notably I.3.143–6, I.4.1–9, I.5.23–4, I.7.58–9, II.1.4–11, 13–14, II.2.2–7, 21–4, II.3.55–63, III.1.43–51, 74–86, III.4.18–21) most modern editors rearrange the lines in order to approximate more closely regular iambic pentameter. See Appendix A.

143 **single state of man** The nature of man is compared to a nation (as in *Julius Caesar*, II.1.65–8), which internal disturbances may reduce to impotence.

150–1 **Come . . . day** That is, even the roughest day must come to an end. This fatalistic thought is relevant to Macbeth's previous aside.

Act I, Scene 4

20–1 **That . . . mine** That I might have been able to make my thanks and reward proportionate to your desert.

21 **I have** Such contractions as 'I've' were common in Elizabethan speech, but are not always indicated in the spelling. Other examples will be found in I.7.29–59, and elsewhere.

41 **Prince of Cumberland** A Scottish title corresponding to Prince of Wales in England.

46 **The rest . . . for you** Any relaxation of the effort to serve you is in reality a greater effort.

Act I, Scene 5

23–6 **Thou'dst have . . . undone** That is, Macbeth would have the crown, which demands that he murder in order to have it; and murder is what he rather fears to do than wishes undone.

39 **raven** The raven's croaking was traditionally associated with gloom and misfortune.

47–8 **keep . . . it** Peaceably intervene between my purpose and its accomplishment.

64 **To beguile the time** *The time* means here 'the world' or 'the present age'; hence, 'to deceive the world.'

Act I, Scene 6

SD **torches** Torches were often used to indicate that the scene took place at night, though the stage of the Elizabethan public theater, lighted by daylight, was necessarily bright. In this scene Duncan approaches the castle gate in the evening. It is light enough for him to see the building and the birds, but the torches remind us that night, called upon by Lady Macbeth in the preceding scene, is falling.

4 **martlet** In Shakespeare's day *martlet* often meant the house

martin, which was supposed to build its nest only in 'fair houses.'

11–14 The love . . . trouble Duncan means that just as we gratefully accept the trouble to which our friends put us as a sign of their love, so Lady Macbeth should thank him for the troublesome visit he is paying her.

23 purveyor An officer whose duty was to ride ahead and make necessary arrangements.

Act I, Scene 7

4 his surcease Probably Duncan's death; possibly the arresting of the consequence.

5–7 here . . . come That is, we'd enjoy the profits of crime in this present life and take our chances on the next life.

8 have judgment That is, we may be punished here by those who follow our example.

22–3 heavens . . . air Psalm 18:10 in the Great Bible (1539) reads: 'He rode upon the Cherubins and dyd flye: he came flyenge with the wynges of the wynde.'

27–8 Vaulting ambition . . . on th' other Ambition, like an overeager horseman, vaults over the saddle and falls on the other side of the horse. The word 'side,' which would fill out the meter of the line, may have dropped out.

45 cat i' th' adage 'The cat would eat fish and would not wet her feet.'

47 do Lady Macbeth's reply makes Macbeth's implication clear: to do more than becomes a man is to behave like a beast. The sense of the context thus justifies the emendation.

60 sticking-place The metaphor is that of a crossbow, the cord of which must be screwed up to the notch where it sticks.

65–7 memory . . . only In Elizabethan physiology memory was thought of as a sort of guard, prepared to warn the brain of attack. It was supposed to be lodged at the base of the skull, reason occupying the upper part. If memory is overcome by fumes of wine rising from the stomach, no warning is given, and the fumes rise to fill the receptacle of reason.

Act II, Scene 1

17–19 Being . . . wrought Our desire to entertain the king was hampered by unpreparedness; otherwise we should have done more.

54 Whose howl's his watch The wolf's howl tells Murder that it is time to act.

55 Tarquin's See Shakespeare's *The Rape of Lucrece*.

Act II, Scene 2

4 bellman A bellman was customarily sent to condemned prisoners the night before their execution.

14SD Enter Macbeth F gives Macbeth's entrance before his speech, 'Who's there?' but this is clearly given offstage.

Act II, Scene 3

4 farmer He had hoarded grain to sell at high prices in a famine; the prospect of a plentiful crop confronted him with ruin.

5–6 Come in, time-server It is logical to expect a phrase here to parallel the later 'come in, equivocator' and 'Come in, tailor.' F's *Come in time* is incomprehensible. J. Dover Wilson, who suggests the emendation adopted here, in his edition of *Macbeth* (Cambridge, Cambridge University Press, 1951, pp. 125–6) says, 'My guess is "come in, time-server," an epithet appropriate to all farmers, who must serve Time in its changes of season and caprices of weather, and to this farmer in its special sense of one who adapts his conduct to the time with an eye to the main chance . . .'

8 equivocator Presumably a reference to Henry Garnet, a Jesuit tried and condemned in 1600 for complicity in the Gunpowder Plot. After perjuring himself at the trial, he defended his conduct on the grounds that equivocation was justifiable in certain circumstances.

14 stealing . . . hose Trousers (hose) made in the latest French style were so tight-fitting that the tailor got caught in trying to steal cloth as he had done in making the larger ones formerly in fashion. There may be a pun on 'staling' (since *stealing* then had the same pronunciation), 'urinating.'

15 goose Possibly continues the *double entendre* on *stealing*, since *goose* also meant a swelling caused by venereal disease.

4SD Enter Macbeth The entrance of a character is frequently

107

indicated a few lines before his first speech, to give him time to walk across the large platform stage, and to give characters onstage the chance to see him and comment on his arrival.

55–63 The night . . . shake In *Macbeth*, as in many other plays, Shakespeare makes use of the commonly held belief that dire portents and disorders in nature accompany disruptions of the social order, such as the assassination of Duncan.

93SD Enter Macbeth and Lennox F indicates an entrance for Ross here, but it is apparent later (II.4.22 ff) that he has not visited Duncan's chamber.

99 vault Refers both to a wine cellar and to the earth, with the sky as a roof.

119 Unmannerly . . . gore The blood makes *unmannerly* breeches for the daggers, whose proper breeches would be sheathes.

125–6 Where . . . seize us That is, where we may be surprised by fate, hidden in the smallest and least suspected place.

127–9 Our tears . . . motion There has not been time yet to weep for our father's death nor to express our sorrow in action.

129 naked frailties All except Lennox and Macduff are in dressing gowns.

Act II, Scene 4

6 stage The frequent comparison of the world to a stage (see V.5.24–6) had a special appropriateness in the Elizabethan public theater, where the canopy over the stage was called 'the heavens,' while the 'cellarage' beneath it often represented hell.

12 tow'ring . . . place Technical terms in falconry: *towering* means circling upward; *place* is the highest point in the falcon's flight.

Act III, Scene 1

25 Go . . . better Unless my horse goes fast enough to make it unnecessary.

42–7 To make . . . safely thus Neither the lineation nor the punctuation of F makes good sense here. This arrangement of lines was suggested by Kenneth Muir in his edition of *Macbeth* (London, Methuen, 1951).

55–6 **My genius . . . Caesar** See *Antony and Cleopatra*, II.3. 19–22.

131 **perfect spy** Macbeth apparently intends to send someone with these final pieces of information; it is logical to assume that the Third Murtherer of Scene 3 is that person.

Act III, Scene 2

13 **scorch'd** Theobald's 18th-century emendation, *scotch'd*, has become familiar, but is unwarranted; it is merely another spelling of the same word.

39 **copy** May also mean lease, since 'copyhold' was a form of tenure.

43 **shard-borne** It is difficult to tell whether this means 'dung-bred' or 'borne on scaly wings.' The latter seems more probable in this context, which calls attention to the beetle's flight, rather than to its origin.

50 **bond** The prophecy that Banquo's descendants should be kings.

Act III, Scene 4

4–6 **Ourself . . . state** Thrones, covered by a canopy, are set up on a dais for the king and queen, probably on the inner stage. On the platform stage is the table for the guests. Macbeth means to sit there with them, while Lady Macbeth will stay on her canopied throne ('keep her state').

13 **Approaching the door** Just as he is about to sit down, Macbeth sees the murderer at the door upstage, some distance from the table, and goes over to confer with him.

34–6 **The feast . . . welcome** That is, a feast where the usual courtesies of the host are omitted seems like a meal sold at an inn.

38SD **Enter . . . Banquo** The ghost may enter at another door than that where Macbeth has been talking, or rise through a trap door beside the table. Macbeth walks back toward the table, but does not at once see the ghost. He first notes that his place is occupied (l. 47), then, recognizing Banquo, supposes that some-one has perpetrated a grim practical joke. Simon Forman, who saw *Macbeth* at the Globe in 1611, seems to have been particularly impressed by this scene, which he describes in detail (see Appendix A). His statement that the ghost entered when Macbeth stood up to toast Banquo has puzzled some editors, but the explanation is simple. Forman apparently remembered the second appearance of the ghost (l. 88), when Macbeth has finally gone to his place at the table and proposed a toast. As he turns to sit down (l. 93), he sees the ghost again. Forman's account shows clearly that, although the ghost is invisible to all except Macbeth on the stage, it is intended to be seen by the audience.

38 remembrancer The word was used as a title for certain officers of the Exchequer, such as The King's Remembrancer.

68 stool The stool was the normal seat for rich and poor in Elizabethan England. Chairs, which were very rare, were reserved for the highest ranking persons present.

71–3 If charnel houses . . . kites That is, it may be safer to let kites (birds of prey) eat dead bodies to prevent them from returning to haunt us.

101 Hyrcan Hyrcania, south of the Caspian Sea, is often mentioned in classical literature as the habitat of tigers.

112–13 You . . . owe You make me feel unfamiliar with my own disposition.

119 Stand . . . going Don't stand on ceremony, the correct order of precedence, etc.

124 understood relations Relations as understood by a soothsayer.

Act III, Scene 5

Scene 5 This scene was probably added by Thomas Middleton or some other contemporary of Shakespeare. The songs indicated in the stage directions here and in IV.1 are found in full in Middleton's *The Witch*. The exact relationship of the two plays has never been determined. See IV.1.39–43 N.

33SD Sing within The second part of this stage direction, *Sing within, 'Come away, come away,'* etc., is printed in F at the end of Heccat's speech. This may indicate that the song is to continue after being interrupted by two spoken lines. Such an arrangement is easy to imagine, since the song, as we have it in *The Witch* (III.3), is in dialogue form, beginning:

110

Come away: Come away: ⎫
Heccat: Heccat, Come away ⎭ *in ye aire.*

(See Malone Society Reprint, Oxford, Oxford University Press, 1950, p. 57.) Heccat answers, 'I come, I come,' but she might very well give this answer after ll. 34–5, and then proceed with the rest of the song. Davenant arranged the stage business in this way in his adaptation, which was published in 1674 with the full text of the song.

34–5 Hark . . . for me Heccat's words suggest that the attendant spirit appears in a car suspended on ropes and possibly wrapped in some light cloth (the 'foggy cloud'). At the end of the song Heccat gets into the car, and it is drawn up into 'the heavens.'

Act III, Scene 6

Scene 6 In this scene Lennox and the other Lord describe the results of the action against Macduff planned by Macbeth in III.4. Macduff has already had time to get to England, though the following scene, IV.1, supposedly occurs the day after III.4. There is no logical explanation for this discrepancy.

30 pray . . . upon his aid *Upon* seems to have the force here of 'relying on.' Shakespeare may have had in mind the expression, 'pray in aid,' meaning 'claim assistance' (to which one has some right).

35 Free . . . knives That is, free our feasts and banquets from bloody knives.

43 clogs The messenger is embarrassed by the answer Macduff makes him return; he is fearful of Macbeth's reaction to it.

Act IV, Scene 1

2 hedge-pig In I.1 the Second Witch's familiar is a toad.

23 mummy Embalmed human flesh and powders or liquids made from it, all known as *mummy*, were used in medicine and were also thought to have great magical power.

23 maw and gulf Both words mean 'stomach'; *gulf*, by suggesting a yawning chasm, emphasizes the voracious appetite of the shark.

38SD **Enter Heccat . . . Witches** The appearance of Heccat and three more witches was probably a non-Shakespearean addition to the play (see III.5 N). No exit is indicated for Heccat but since she has no lines after l. 43, she probably leaves at this point. The other witches may remain to join in the dance (doubtless another addition) after l. 131.

39–43 **O, well done . . . you put in** These lines, like many in III.5, are iambic tetrameter, whereas the witches elsewhere speak in trochaic tetrameter. This discrepancy is one reason for doubting that they originally belonged in the play. The reference to 'elves and fairies' also strikes a false note.

67SD **First Apparition** Each of the three apparitions rises and then descends through a trap door, probably on the inner stage. The significance of the *Armed Head* is disputable. Some have thought it prefigured the head of Macbeth, cut off by Macduff at the end of the play. It is more likely that it represents Macduff, the adversary of whom Macbeth is here told to beware. As George Lyman Kittredge has pointed out in his edition of *Macbeth* (Boston, Ginn and Co., 1939, p. 189), each of the other apparitions represents a person dangerous to Macbeth; the first apparition should set the pattern. Kittredge also notes that 'the First Apparition should not represent something that comes to pass later than the events foretold by the Second and Third.'

75SD **Second Apparition** Represents Macduff: see V.7.44–5.

85 SD **Third Apparition** The child is presumably Malcolm, holding a tree to represent the stratagem by which his army approaches Dunsinane: see V.4.4–7.

93SD **Descend** An imperative verb is often used in Elizabethan stage directions.

96 **head** Macbeth presumably refers again to Macduff, whose 'armed head' is the one potential threat to his security. F's *Rebellious dead* has been interpreted by some as evidence that Macbeth is thinking of Banquo, whom he mentions at l. 101; but *Rebellious dead* would seem to be plural, and, in any case, Banquo cannot well be called 'rebellious.' It is more likely that *head* was mistakenly printed as *dead*.

97 **Birnam** The modern form of this name, suggested by F *Byrnam* at its first mention (l. 92), has been kept throughout.

though F spells it more often with a final n (as here) or ne. Deviations from F's spelling of the name are not elsewhere noted.

105 sinks that cauldron The cauldron is lowered by a machine through one of the trap doors.

110 SD A show of eight Kings The stage direction as printed in F, *A shew of eight Kings, and Banquo last, with a glasse in his hand*, contradicts l. 118, where it is clear that the last king carries the glass. Various reconstructions of the stage business have been made, with corresponding emendations of the text. The emendation adopted here suits the following hypotheses: It seems likely that the kings enter at one side of the stage and move across to the other in a dignified and spectacular procession. They probably remain in sight until l. 123, where Banquo 'points at them,' after which they may *vanish* with him in a stage mist, as the witches do. Since they are all Banquo's descendants, he may precede them onto the stage, standing aside where Macbeth can note their resemblance to him (l. 111).

However this *show* was staged, it is certain that it had a special topical importance as a compliment to King James, before whom the play was probably first given (see Henry N. Paul, *The Royal Play of Macbeth*, New York, Macmillan, 1950, pp. 162–82, 317–31). The Stuarts claimed their descent from Banquo, and James was the ninth Stuart sovereign. His mother, Mary, Queen of Scots, whom Queen Elizabeth forced to abdicate, was the eighth. Faced with the delicate problem of presenting this controversial member of the family, Shakespeare may, as Paul suggests (p. 179) have created a deliberate ambiguity about the eighth 'king,' who may have appeared on the stage heavily shrouded and carrying the glass before his face. In this way various members of the audience would be free to assume that the mysterious figure represented the ill-fated Mary (the eighth 'king' in the generic sense of the word) or her fortunate son (the eighth male sovereign), who could not, however, be plainly depicted without *lèse majesté*. Shakespeare may have seen the drawing of the Stuart genealogical tree published during Mary's lifetime in John Leslie's *De Origine, Moribus, et Rebus Gestis Scotorum* (Rome, 1578), showing the series of 'eight kings' descended from Banquo. On this tree, Mary is the eighth.

118 **glass** Presumably a magic glass in which the future can be seen.

120 **twofold . . . scepters** The ball is part of the royal regalia; *twofold* probably refers to England and Scotland, united under James; the *treble scepters* probably indicate that James is king of England, Scotland, and Ireland.

124–31 **Ay, sir . . . his welcome pay** The meter and the spirit of these lines again seem out of keeping. They were probably added with the Heccat material.

144–5 **The flighty . . . it** Unless intentions are translated into deeds, they remain forever out of reach.

Act IV, Scene 2

83 **shag-hair'd** Refers to the long, unkempt hair of the Elizabethan ruffian.

Act IV, Scene 3

15 **discern** Macduff may learn something about Macbeth through Malcolm's plight, and he may even learn the *wisdom* of betraying Malcolm to Macbeth. The unexpected suggestion of the latter part of the sentence makes it at first obscure. Most editors change *discern* to *deserve*, but by this emendation the second half of the sentence is cast adrift: Macduff doesn't *deserve* wisdom.

98–100 **Pour . . . earth** *Concord*, *peace*, and *unity* have not only their general significance here but also a special topical reference, since these were the avowed goals of James I's foreign and domestic policy.

136–7 **the chance . . . quarrel** That is, may the chance of good fortune equal the justness of our cause.

142 **stay his cure** Edward the Confessor was thought to be able to heal 'the king's evil' (scrofula) by his touch. The passage is presumably an indirect compliment to James I, who claimed the same healing power.

170 **ecstasy** Probably alludes to the sham fits of people pretending to be 'possessed.' Several such cases were known in Shakespeare's day.

221 **dispute it** Sometimes interpreted as 'contend with your

sorrow,' but notice that Malcolm has just urged Macduff to
express his sorrow (l. 209).

Act V, Scene 1

27 **are** The plural, though not strictly grammatical, is probably
due to the thought of the two eyes, both unseeing.

Act V, Scene 2

30 **sovereign flower** Suggests both 'flower of true sovereignty'
(as opposed to usurping weeds) and 'healing, restorative flower'
(as opposed to noxious weeds).

Act V, Scene 3

21 **cheer** In Shakespeare's day, as still in many dialects, 'chair'
had the same pronunciation. There is therefore a pun on 'chair'
which relates *cheer* to *disseat*.

55 **cyme** Probably refers to the 'cymes' or tops of the colewort,
often taken as a cathartic. May be a misprint for 'cinne,' another
spelling of 'senna,' also a cathartic.

Act V, Scene 4

19–20 **Thoughts** . . . **arbitrate** That is, optimistic speculation
is mere wishful thinking; battle will decide the issues.

Act V, Scene 7

2 **bearlike** . . . **course** The comparison is to the popular
Elizabethan sport of bear-baiting, in which a bear, tied to a post,
was attacked by dogs. A *course* was one round or bout.

13SD **Exit** Here, or possibly after l. 23, the body of Young
Siward must be removed, for at l. 73 we learn that he has been
'brought off the field.' Whether or not the body is still onstage
when Macduff enters, it is clear that he does not see it, nor does
the elder Siward when he enters (l. 23). The entire scene is an
excellent example of the fluidity of Elizabethan staging. Different localities are suggested in rapid succession by the use of
different parts of the stage. Macduff apparently enters at some
distance from the place where Macbeth has killed Young Siward;
when Malcolm and the elder Siward enter, they probably head

for the inner stage, which may represent the gates of the castle; when Macbeth re-enters, the action is presumably away from the inner stage again, suggesting another part of the field of battle; the entrance at l. 63 may be in the inner stage to indicate that it is inside the castle. Because of the size and the facilities of the stage this panoramic action can be continuous and the pace rapid.

29SD **Enter Macbeth** Many editors begin a new scene here, and some begin another new scene at 63SD. The explanation in the preceding note should make it clear why such scene division was unnecessary in writing for the Elizabethan stage.

APPENDIX A

Text and Date

The Tragedie of Macbeth was first printed in the Folio of 1623, the First Folio. This is the only authoritative text, and is consequently the basis of the present edition. From the early 18th century to the present time many editors, feeling that the Folio text was seriously corrupt, have altered it extensively. The main reasons for this feeling are, first, that the play is abnormally short, suggesting that it was cut; second, that certain passages presenting Heccat (III.5; IV.1.39–43, 124–31), stylistically different from the rest of the play, seem to have been interpolated; and, third, that the lineation of the play is often markedly irregular. Most critics agree that the shortness may be due in part to the special requirements of a court performance, but it cannot be proved that there was a much longer version which was drastically cut, as some have suspected. In fact, it is difficult to imagine what of any importance is missing from the play as it stands. As A. C. Bradley pointed out long ago in his *Shakespearean Tragedy* (London, Macmillan, 1912, pp. 468–9): (1) 'there is no internal evidence of the omission of anything essential to the plot,' (2) Simon Forman, who saw the play in 1611 (see below) mentions nothing we do not find in the Folio; and (3) if extensive cuts were made, their location is extremely puzzling. The question is complicated by the virtual certainty that Shakespeare did not leave the play in its present form. The Heccat passages, referred to above, not only stand out stylistically, but seem to relate *Macbeth* to *The Witch*, a manuscript play by Thomas Middleton, in which Heccat appears, singing two songs indicated in the stage directions of *Macbeth* (III.5.33, IV.1.43). The exact relationship of these plays is uncertain, but it is probable that someone, possibly Middleton himself, added the Heccat passages in the course of revising Shakespeare's play. Although this speculation opens the further possibility that the entire play was substantially altered at the time of this revision, a conservative view limits the changes to the relatively brief interpolations.

It is possible, then, that neither the first nor the second reason

117

for suspecting widespread corruption is valid. Recent editors, such as J. Dover Wilson and Kenneth Muir, argue against the earlier, pessimistic view. The irregular lineation of the Folio, however, presents a difficult problem. If it is not due to the hand of an unskillful reviser, it may be explained as the fantasy of a compositor or as an indication of how the lines should be read. Though I do not brush aside the possibility that the compositor (or a transcriber of the manuscript) rearranged Shakespeare's lines, the alternative explanation seems to me to deserve more consideration than it has been given. For example, Wilson[1] cites the end of II.2 as a place where the compositors 'have obviously been monkeying with the verse-lining . . . in order to fill up their columns.' It may be so, but can we be certain that the Folio printing does not indicate the pauses occasioned by the knocking at the gate and by the anxiety it arouses in Lady Macbeth and Macbeth? A pause between Macbeth's last two lines seems a necessity, and in each of the other cases where these half-lines appear as separate lines, a marked pause might create an appropriate effect. If the half-lines are combined, as is usually done, the indication of such effects is lost. Here and in a few comparable situations I have retained the separate lines, but have introduced modern echeloning. Another example of a sort of punctuation by line-division is provided by III.2.22–3, which most editors print as one line. This alteration not only obscures what may again be the indication of a pause, but suggests that *ecstasy* should be crowded into one foot so as to make room in the line for 'Duncan is in his grave.' As they are printed in the Folio, both of these short lines are made up of three feet, and the rhythm and meaning are better served by reading them in that way. Accentuation is adversely affected in another instance, III.1.77–8, printed by most editors:

> which held you
> So under fortune, which you thought had been
> Our innocent self.

1. *Macbeth*, Cambridge, Cambridge University Press, 1951, pp. 90–1.

The Folio arrangement, reprinted in this text, suggests the accentuation:

Which you thought had been our innocent self.

This reading, with its heavy emphasis on Macbeth's deceptive portrayal of himself, seems to me a good one; it is surely not indicated by the alternative arrangement. One more instance of what may be punctuation by irregular line-division is II.1.8–10. It is natural for Banquo to pause after the word *sleep* before uttering his anguished prayer. Though l. 9 has six feet and l. 10 only four, no rearrangement is entirely satisfactory, and the lines as they stand correspond to a natural musical phrasing.

In the face of such evidence we cannot assume that we shall be getting back to what Shakespeare wrote by rearranging the lines in the closest approximation to iambic pentameter. Since the contrary assumption, that the Folio is always right, is also unwarranted, each irregularity must be considered separately. My aim has been to reproduce the Folio lineation except where I could find no *raison d'être* for an irregularity, or where one could be corrected easily without altering the rhythm or meaning. For example, the Folio prints I.3.133–5 thus:

This supernaturall solliciting
Cannot be ill; cannot be good.
If ill? why hath it giuen me earnest of successe,

This division might be defended as logical, but no damage is done to a good reading of the lines by adding the first foot of l. 135 to the end of l. 134, making them both normal five-foot lines. In some instances, such as III.1.86–92, the familiar modern rearrangement seems a definite improvement over the Folio's senseless irregularity. Here is the passage as the Folio gives it:

Macb. I did so:
And went further, which is now
Our point of second meeting.
Doe you finde your patience so predominant,
In your nature, that you can let this goe?
Are you so Gospell'd, to pray for this good man,

119

> And for his Issue, whose heauie hand
> Hath bow'd you to the Graue, and begger'd
> Yours for euer?

This erratic lineation in no way clarifies the meaning of the passage, nor does it correspond to any conceivable speech rhythm. In such instances I have reproduced a regularization of the lines.

My conclusion is that the case against the irregular lineation of the Folio is not proven. In a large number of passages, therefore, I have preferred to accept the Folio arrangement as possibly deliberate and meaningful. While there is no guarantee that Shakespeare wrote the lines this way, there is at least a fair chance that they were spoken this way, whereas the regularizations often represent only the prosody of an 18th-century editor. The argument for the procedure I have adopted is strengthened by the fact that comparable irregularities of lineation occur in *Coriolanus* and *Antony and Cleopatra*, which are thought to have been set up from Shakespeare's own manuscripts. I should point out here that because I have not kept the modern regularizations, the line-numbering of this edition often differs slightly from that of the Globe edition, on which many references are based.

There is little obscurity in *Macbeth*. In a very few instances, where it seemed essential for the understanding of a passage, I have accepted emendations, recording the divergence from the Folio at the foot of the page. I have rejected two emendations which have become so familiar that the original forms will shock many readers. *Scorch'd* (III.2.13) is a good word, and has been accepted by several modern editors in preference to Theobald's unnecessary emendation, *scotch'd*. Theobald is also responsible for *weird*, instead of which I have kept *weyard*, the form occurring most often in the Folio. The spelling *weird* never occurs there, and Theobald's diaeresis is an unsatisfactory means of indicating the two syllables clearly required by the meter. Except in such instances as this, where an archaic spelling is a necessary indication of pronunciation, I have used modern American spelling. In punctuating, I have tried to give the modern equivalents of the Elizabethan marks.

The first recorded performance of *Macbeth* is that which the astrologer, Dr. Simon Forman, attended on April 20, 1611. Though his reference to 'women feiries or Nimphes' suggests that he refreshed his memory of the play by reading in Holinshed's *Chronicle*, his account of the performance is extremely interesting as showing what particularly struck one contemporary spectator:

In Mackbeth at the glob[2] 1610 [3] the 20 of aprill [Saturday[4]]. ther was to be obserued firste howe Mackbeth and Bancko 2 noble men[5] of Scotland Ridinge thorowe a wod the[r] stode befor them 3 women feiries or Nimphes And Saluted Mackbeth sayinge: 3 tyms vnto him. Haille mackbeth. king of Codor[6] for thou shalt be a kinge but shalt beget No kinges. &c. then said Bancko What all to mackbeth And nothing to me. Yes said the nimphes Haille to thee Banko thou shalt beget king*es*. yet be no kinge And so they dep*ar*ted & cam to the Courte of Scotland to Dunkin king of Scot*es* and yt was in the dais of Edward the Confessor. And Dunkin bad them both kindly wellcom. And made Mackbeth forth with Prince of Northumberland. and sent him hom to his own castell and appointed mackbeth to prouid for him for he wold Sup with him the next dai at night. & did soe. And mackebeth contrived to kill Dunkin. & thorowe the p*er*suasion of his wife did that night Murder the kinge in his own Castell beinge his guest And ther were many prodigies seen that night & the dai before. And when Mack Beth had murdred the kinge the blod on his hand*es* could not be washed of by Any means. nor from his wiues hand*es* w*hich* handled the bluddi daggers in hiding them By w*hich* means they became both moch amazed & affronted. the murder being knowen Dunkins 2 sonns fled the on to England the [other to] Walles to saue them selues. they beinge fled they were supposed guilty of the murder of their father which was nothinge so— Then was Mackbeth. Crowned kinge and then he for feare of Banko his old Companion that he should beget king*es* but be no kinge him self. he contriued the death of Banko and caused him to be Murdred on the way as he Rode The next night beinge at supper w*ith* his noble men whom he had bid to a feaste to the w*hich* also Banco should haue com. he began to speake of Noble Banco and to wish that he wer ther. And as he thus did standing vp to drincke a Carouse to him. the ghoste of Banco came and sate down in his cheier behind him. And he turninge About to sit down Again sawe the goste of banco which fronted him so. that he fell in to a great passion of fear & fury. Vtteringe many wordes about his murder by which when they hard that Banco was Murdred they Suspected Mackbet.

Then Mack Dove fled to England to the kinges sonn. And soe they Raised an Army and cam into scotland. and at dun ston Anyse over thrue Mackbet. In the meantyme whille Macdouee was in England Mackbet slewe Mackdoues wife & children. and after in the battelle mackdoue slewe mackbet.

Obserue Also howe Mackbetes quen did Rise in the night in her slepe & walke and talked and confessed all & the docter noted her wordes.[7]

That the performance seen by Forman was not the first is suggested by what see a to be topical allusions in the play to events of 1606, such as the apparent reference to Garnet in II.3.8. *Macbeth* may have been given at Hampton Court before James I and his royal guest, Christian IV of Denmark, on August 7, 1606; Shakespeare may even have written the play specifically for this occasion.[8] From various bits of evidence it seems most likely that *Macbeth* belongs to the year 1606.

Any editor of Shakespeare is enormously indebted to his predecessors. I wish to acknowledge in particular my debt to Mark Harvey Liddell (New York, Doubleday, Page, 1903), George Lyman Kittredge (Boston, Ginn, 1939), J. Dover Wilson (Cambridge, Cambridge University Press, 1947), and Kenneth Muir (London, Methuen, 1951). I am grateful for innumerable suggestions from the general editors of the Yale Shakespeare, Professors Helge Kökeritz and Charles T. Prouty.

2. Miswritten 'glod.'

3. A slip for '1611,' as is clear from other entries in the MS.

4. Represented by an astronomical sign for Saturn.

5. Italicized letters indicate expansions of MS contractions.

6. Miswritten 'Codon.'

7. See *Macbeth*, ed. G. L. Kittredge, pp. 240–1; E. K. Chambers, *William Shakespeare*, Oxford, Clarendon Press, 1930, 2, 337–8.

8. Henry N. Paul, *The Royal Play of Macbeth* (New York, Macmillan, 1950, pp. 317–31), adduces persuasive evidence to support this hypothesis.

APPENDIX B

Sources

Shakespeare's chief source for *Macbeth* was the second edition (1587) of Raphael Holinshed's *Chronicles of England, Scotland, and Ireland*. The excerpts from 'The Historie of Scotland' printed below illustrate how Shakespeare put together details from various sections of this work. He obviously read in the pages preceding the account of Macbeth about the murder of King Duff by Donwald, and about the sleeplessness of King Kenneth, tormented by guilt after he had murdered his nephew:

> But Donwald, not forgetting the reproch which his linage had susteined by the execution of those his kinsmen, whome the king for a spectacle to the people had caused to be hanged, could not but shew manifest tokens of great griefe at home amongst his familie: which his wife perceiuing, ceassed not to trauell with him, till she vnderstood what the cause was of his displeasure. Which at length when she had learned by his owne relation, she as one that bare no lesse malice in hir heart towards the king, for the like cause on hir behalfe, than hir husband did for his friends, counselled him (sith the king oftentimes vsed to lodge in his house without anie gard about him, other than the garrison of the castell, which was wholie at his commandement) to make him awaie, and shewed him the meanes wherby he might soonest accomplish it.

> Donwald thus being the more kindled in wrath by the words of his wife, determined to follow hir aduise in the execution of so heinous an act. Whervpon deuising with himselfe for a while, which way hee might best accomplish his curssed intent, at length gat opportunitie, and sped his purpose as followeth. It chanced that the king vpon the daie before he purposed to depart foorth of the castell, was long in his oratorie at his praiers, and there continued till it was late in the night. At the last, comming foorth, he called such afore him as had faithfullie serued him in pursute and apprehension of the rebels, and giuing them heartie thanks, he bestowed sundrie honorable gifts

123

amongst them, of the which number Donwald was one, as he that had beene euer accounted a most faithfull seruant to the king.

At length, hauing talked with them a long time, he got him into his priuie chamber, onelie with two of his chamberlains, who hauing brought him to bed, came foorth againe, and then fell to banketting with Donwald and his wife, who had prepared diuerse delicate dishes, and sundrie sorts of drinks for their reare supper or collation, wherat they sate vp so long, till they had charged their stomachs with such full gorges, that their heads were no sooner got to the pillow, but asleepe they were so fast, that a man might haue remooued the chamber ouer them, sooner than to haue awaked them out of their droonken sleepe.

Then Donwald, though he abhorred the act greatlie in heart, yet through instigation of his wife hee called foure of his seruants vnto him (whome he had made priuie to his wicked intent before, and framed to his purpose with large gifts) and now declaring vnto them, after what sort they should worke the feat, they gladlie obeied his instructions, & speedilie going about the murther, they enter the chamber (in which the king laie) a little before cocks crow, where they secretlie cut his throte as he lay sleeping, without anie buskling at all: and immediatlie by a posterne gate they caried foorth the dead bodie into the fields . . .

Donwald, about the time that the murther was in dooing, got him amongst them that kept the watch, and so continued in companie with them all the residue of the night. But in the morning when the noise was raised in the kings chamber how the king was slaine, his bodie conueied awaie, and the bed all beraied with bloud; he with the watch ran thither, as though he had knowne nothing of the matter, and breaking into the chamber, and finding cakes of bloud in the bed, and on the floore about the sides of it, he foorthwith slue the chamberleins, as guiltie of that heinous murther, and then like a mad man running to and fro, he ransacked euerie corner within the castell, as though it had beene to haue seene if he might haue found either the bodie, or anie of the murtherers hid in anie priuie place: but at length comming to the posterne gate, and finding it open, he burdened the chamberleins, whome he had slaine, with all the fault, they hauing the keies of the gates committed to their keeping all the night, and therefore it could not be otherwise (said he) but that they were of counsell in the committing of that most detestable murther.

Finallie, such was his ouer earnest diligence in the seuere inquisition and triall of the offendors heerein, that some of the lords began to mislike the matter, and to smell foorth shrewd tokens, that he should not be altogither cleare himselfe. But for so much as they were in that countrie, where he had the whole rule, what by reason of his friends and authoritie togither, they doubted to vtter what they thought, till time and place should better serue therevnto, and heerevpon got them awaie euerie man to his home. For the space of six moneths togither, after this heinous murther thus committed, there appeered no sunne by day, nor moone by night in anie part of the realme, but still was the skie couered with continuall clouds, and sometimes such outragious winds arose, with lightenings and tempests, that the people were in great feare of present destruction. . . .

Monstrous sights also that were seene within the Scotish kingdome that yeere were these: horsses in Louthian, being of singular beautie and swiftnesse, did eate their owne flesh, and would in no wise taste anie other meate. In Angus there was a gentlewoman brought foorth a child without eies, nose, hand, or foot. There was a sparhawke also strangled by an owle. Neither was it anie lesse woonder that the sunne, as before is said, was continuallie couered with clouds for six moneths space. But all men vnderstood that the abhominable murther of king Duffe was the cause heereof . . . (Pp. 150–2.)

Thus might he seeme happie to all men, hauing the loue both of his lords and commons: but yet to himselfe he seemed most vnhappie, as he that could not but still liue in continuall feare, least his wicked practise concerning the death of Malcolme Duffe should come to light and knowledge of the world. For so commeth it to passe, that such as are pricked in conscience for anie secret offense committed, haue euer an vnquiet mind. And (as the fame goeth) it chanced that a voice was heard as he was in bed in the night time to take his rest, vttering vnto him these or the like woords in effect: 'Thinke not Kenneth that the wicked slaughter of Malcolme Duffe by thee contriued, is kept secret from the knowledge of the eternall God: thou art he that didst conspire the innocents death, enterprising by traitorous meanes to doo that to thy neighbour, which thou wouldest haue reuenged by cruell punishment in anie of thy subiects, if it had beene offered to thy selfe. It shall therefore come to passe, that both thou thy selfe, and thy issue, through the iust vengeance of almightie God, shall suffer woorthie punishment, to the infamie of thy house and familie for euermore. For euen at this present are there in hand secret practises to dispatch both thee and thy issue out of the waie, that other maie inioy this kingdome which thou doost indeuour to assure vnto thine issue.'

The king, with this voice being striken into great dread and terror, passed that night without anie sleepe comming in his eies. (P. 158.)

Ten pages later comes the story of Duncan's succession to the throne:

After Malcolme succeeded his nephue Duncane the sonne of his daughter Beatrice: for Malcolme had two daughters, the one which was this Beatrice, being giuen in mariage vnto one Abbanath Crinen, a man of great nobilitie, and thane of the Iles and west parts of Scotland, bare of that mariage the foresaid Duncane; the other called Doada, was maried vnto Sinell the thane of Glammis, by whom she had issue one Makbeth a valiant gentleman, and one that if he had not beene somewhat cruell of nature, might haue beene thought most woorthie the gouernement of a realme. On the other part, Duncane was so soft and gentle of nature, that the people wished the inclinations and maners of these two cousins to haue beene so tempered and interchangeablie bestowed betwixt them, that where the one had too much of clemencie, and the other of crueltie, the meane vertue betwixt these two extremities might haue reigned by indifferent partition in them both, so should Duncane haue proued a woorthie king, and Makbeth an excellent capteine.

Holinshed then gives a lengthy account of the rebellion of Makdowald (Shakespeare's 'merciless Macdonwald'), and the wars against Sueno of Norway and Canute of England, in all of which Macbeth and Banquo fought victoriously for Duncan. The three actions are combined in the account given in I.2. Next comes the introduction of Macbeth's ambition for the throne:

And these were the warres that Duncane had with forren enimies, in the seuenth yeere of his reigne. Shortlie after happened a strange and vncouth woonder, which afterward was the cause of much trouble in the realme of Scotland, as ye shall after heare. It fortuned as Makbeth and Banquho iournied towards Fores, where the king then laie, they went sporting by the waie togither without other companie, saue onelie themselues, passing thorough the woods and fields, when suddenlie in the middest of a laund, there met them three women in strange and wild apparell, resembling creatures of elder world, whome when they attentiuelie beheld, woondering much at the sight, the first of them spake and said; 'All haile Makbeth, thane of Glammis' (for he had latelie entered into that dignitie and office by the death of his father Sinell). The second of them said; 'Haile Makbeth thane of Cawder.' But the third said; 'All haile Makbeth that heereafter shalt be king of Scotland.'

Then Banquho; 'What manner of women (saith he) are you, that seeme so little fauourable vnto me, whereas to my fellow heere, besides high offices, ye assigne also the kingdome, appointing foorth nothing for me at all?' 'Yes (saith the first of them) we promise greater benefits vnto thee, than vnto him, for he shall reigne in deed, but with an vnluckie end: neither shall he leaue anie issue behind him to succeed in his place, where contrarilie thou in deed shalt not reigne at all, but of thee those shall be borne which shall gouerne the Scotish kingdome by long order of continuall descent.' Herewith the foresaid women vanished immediatlie out of their sight. This was reputed at the first but some vaine fantasticall illusion by Mack-

beth and Banquho, insomuch that Banquho would call Mackbeth in iest, king of Scotland; and Mackbeth againe would call
him in sport likewise, the father of manie kings. But afterwards
the common opinion was, that these women were either the
weird sisters, that is (as ye would say) the goddesses of destinie,
or else some nymphs or feiries, indued with knowledge of prophesie by their necromanticall science, bicause euerie thing
came to passe as they had spoken. For shortlie after, the thane
of Cawder being condemned at Fores of treason against the
king committed; his lands, liuings, and offices were giuen of the
kings liberalitie to Mackbeth.

The same night after, at supper, Banquho iested with him and
said; Now Mackbeth thou hast obteined those things which the
two former sisters prophesied, there remaineth onelie for thee
to purchase that which the third said should come to passe.
Wherevpon Mackbeth reuoluing the thing in his mind, began
euen then to deuise how he might atteine to the kingdome: but
yet he thought with himselfe that he must tarie a time, which
should aduance him thereto (by the diuine prouidence) as it
had come to passe in his former preferment. But shortlie after
it chanced that king Duncane, hauing two sonnes by his wife
which was the daughter of Siward earle of Northumberland,
he made the elder of them called Malcolme prince of Cumberland, as it were thereby to appoint him his successor in the
kingdome, immediatlie after his deceasse. Mackbeth sore troubled herewith, for that he saw by this means his hope sore
hindered (where, by the old lawes of the realme, the ordinance
was, that if he that should succeed were not of able age to take
the charge vpon himselfe, he that was next of bloud vnto him
should be admitted) he began to take counsell how he might
vsurpe the kingdome by force, hauing a iust quarell so to doo
(as he tooke the matter) for that Duncane did what in him lay
to defraud him of all maner of title and claime, which he might
in time to come, pretend vnto the crowne.

The woords of the three weird sisters also (of whom before ye
haue heard) greatlie incouraged him herevnto, but speciallie
his wife lay sore vpon him to attempt the thing, as she that was

verie ambitious, burning in vnquenchable desire to beare the
name of a queene. At length therefore, communicating his pur-
posed intent with his trustie friends, amongst whome Banquho
was the chiefest, vpon confidence of their promised aid, he slue
the king at Enuerns, or (as some say) at Botgosuane, in the
sixt yeare of his reigne. Then hauing a companie about him of
such as he had made priuie to his enterprise, he caused himselfe
to be proclamed king, and foorthwith went vnto Scone, where
(by common consent) he receiued the inuesture of the kingdome according to the accustomed maner. The bodie of Duncane was first conueied vnto Elgine, & there buried in kinglie
wise; but afterwards it was remoued and conueied vnto Colmekill, and there laid in a sepulture amongst his predecessors, in
the yeare after the birth of our Sauiour, 1046.

Malcolme Cammore and Donald Bane the sons of king Duncane, for feare of their liues (which they might well know that
Mackbeth would seeke to bring to end for his more sure con-
firmation in the estate) fled into Cumberland, where Malcolme
remained, till time that saint Edward the sonne of Ethelred
recouered the dominion of England from the Danish power,
the which Edward receiued Malcolme by way of most friendlie
enterteinment: but Donald passed ouer into Ireland, where he
was tenderlie cherished by the king of that land. Mackbeth,
after the departure thus of Duncanes sonnes, vsed great liberalitie towards the nobles of the realme, thereby to win their
fauour, and when he saw that no man went about to trouble
him, he set his whole intention to mainteine iustice, and to
punish all enormities and abuses, which had chanced through
the feeble and slouthfull administration of Duncane. (Pp.
170–1.)

After Holinshed has described some good laws passed by Macbeth at the beginning of his reign, he continues:

These and the like commendable lawes Makbeth caused to be
put as then in vse, gouerning the realme for the space of ten
yeares in equall iustice. But this was but a counterfet zeale of
equitie shewed by him, partlie against his naturall inclination

129

to purchase thereby the fauour of the people. Shortlie after, he began to shew what he was, in stead of equitie practising crueltie. For the pricke of conscience (as it chanceth euer in tyrants, and such as atteine to anie estate by vnrighteous means) caused him euer to feare, least he should be serued of the same cup, as he had ministred to his predecessor. The woords also of the three weird sisters, would not out of his mind, which as they promised him the kingdome, so likewise did they promise it at the same time vnto the posteritie of Banquho. He willed therefore the same Banquho with his sonne named Fleance, to come to a supper that he had prepared for them, which was in deed, as he had deuised, present death at the hands of certeine murderers, whom he hired to execute that deed, appointing them to meete with the same Banquho and his sonne without the palace, as they returned to their lodgings, and there to slea them, so that he would not haue his house slandered, but that in time to come he might cleare himselfe, if anie thing were laid to his charge vpon anie suspicion that might arise.

It chanced yet by the benefit of the darke night, that though the father were slaine, the sonne yet by the helpe of almightie God reseruing him to better fortune, escaped that danger: and afterwards hauing some inkeling (by the admonition of some friends which he had in the court) how his life was sought no lesse than his fathers, who was slaine not by chancemedlie (as by the handling of the matter Makbeth woould haue had it to appeare) but euen vpon a prepensed deuise: wherevpon to auoid further perill he fled into Wales. (P. 172.)

An account of the Stuart dynasty follows. Shakespeare, at a comparable point in his play, introduces the 'show of eight kings.' Holinshed then describes how Macbeth became suspicious of Macduff:

Neither could he afterwards abide to looke vpon the said Mak-duffe, either for that he thought his puissance ouer great; either else for that he had learned of certeine wizzards, in whose words he put great confidence (for that the prophesie had happened

so right, which the three faries or weird sisters had declared
vnto him) how that he ought to take heed of Makduffe, who
in time to come should seeke to destroie him.

And suerlie herevpon had he put Makduffe to death, but that
a certeine witch, whom hee had in great trust, had told that
he should neuer be slaine with man borne of anie woman, nor
vanquished till the wood of Bernane came to the castell of
Dunsinane. By this prophesie Makbeth put all feare out of his
heart, supposing he might doo what he would, without anie
feare to be punished for the same, for by the one prophesie he
beleeued it was vnpossible for anie man to vanquish him, and
by the other vnpossible to slea him. This vaine hope caused
him to doo manie outragious things, to the greeuous oppression
of his subiects. At length Makduffe, to auoid perill of life, pur-
posed with himselfe to passe into England, to procure Malcolme Cammore to claime the crowne of Scotland. But this was
not so secretlie deuised by Makduffe, but that Makbeth had
knowledge giuen him thereof: for kings (as is said) haue sharpe
sight like vnto Lynx, and long ears like vnto Midas. For Makbeth had in euerie noble mans house one slie fellow or other in
fee with him, to reueale all that was said or doone within the
same, by which slight he oppressed the most part of the nobles
of his realme.

Immediatlie then, being aduertised whereabout Makduffe
went, he came hastily with a great power into Fife, and foorthwith besieged the castell where Makduffe dwelled, trusting to
haue found him therein. They that kept the house, without anie
resistance opened the gates, and suffered him to enter, mis-
trusting none euill. But neuerthelesse Makbeth most cruellie
caused the wife and children of Makduffe, with all other whom
he found in that castell, to be slaine. Also he confiscated the
goods of Makduffe, proclamed him traitor, and confined him
out of all the parts of his realme; but Makduffe was alreadie
escaped out of danger, and gotten into England vnto Malcolme
Cammore, to trie what purchase hee might make by means of
his support, to reuenge the slaughter so cruellie executed on his
wife, his children, and other friends. At his comming vnto Mal-

colme, he declared into what great miserie the estate of Scot. land was brought, by the detestable cruelties exercised by the tyrant Makbeth, hauing committed manie horrible slaughters and murders, both as well of the nobles as commons, for the which he was hated right mortallie of all his liege people, desiring nothing more than to be deliuered of that intollerable and most heauie yoke of thraldome, which they susteined at such a caitifes hands.

Malcolme hearing Makduffe's woords, which he vttered in verie lamentable sort, for meere compassion and verie ruth that pearsed his sorowfull hart, bewailing the miserable state of his countrie, he fetched a deepe sigh; which Makduffe perceiuing, began to fall most earnestlie in hand with him, to enterprise the deliuering of the Scotish people out of the hands of so cruell and bloudie a tyrant, as Makbeth by too manie plaine experiments did shew himselfe to be: which was an easie matter for him to bring to passe, considering not onelie the good title he had, but also the earnest desire of the people to haue some occasion ministred, whereby they might be reuenged of those notable iniuries, which they dailie susteined by the outragious crueltie of Makbeths misgouernance. Though Malcolme was verie sorowfull for the oppression of his countriemen the Scots, in maner as Makduffe had declared; yet doubting whether he were come as one that ment vnfeinedlie as he spake, or else as sent from Makbeth to betraie him, he thought to haue some further triall, and therevpon dissembling his mind at the first, he answered as followeth.

'I am trulie verie sorie for the miserie chanced to my countrie of Scotland, but though I haue neuer so great affection to relieue the same, yet by reason of certeine incurable vices, which reigne in me, I am nothing meet thereto. First, such immoderate lust and voluptuous sensualitie (the abhominable founteine of all vices) followeth me, that if I were made king of Scots, I should seeke to defloure your maids and matrones, in such wise that mine intemperancie should be more importable vnto you than the bloudie tyrannie of Makbeth now is.' Heerevnto Makduffe answered: 'This suerlie is a verie euill fault, for

manie noble princes and kings haue lost both liues and king-
domes for the same; neuerthelesse there are women enow in
Scotland, and therefore follow my counsell. Make thy selfe
king, and I shall conueie the matter so wiselie, that thou shalt
be so satisfied at thy pleasure in such secret wise, that no man
shall be aware thereof.'

Then said Malcolme, 'I am also the most auaritious creature
on the earth, so that if I were king, I should seeke so manie
waies to get lands and goods, that I would slea the most part
of all the nobles of Scotland by surmized accusations, to the
end I might inioy their lands, goods, and possessions; and therefore to shew you what mischiefe may insue on you through
mine vnsatiable couetousnes, I will rehearse vnto you a fable.
There was a fox hauing a sore place on him ouerset with a
swarme of flies, that continuallie sucked out hir bloud: and
when one that came by and saw this manner, demanded
whether she would haue the flies driuen beside hir, she answered
no: for if these flies that are alreadie full, and by reason thereof
sucke not verie egerlie, should be chased awaie, other that are
emptie and fellie an hungred, should light in their places, and
sucke out the residue of my bloud farre more to my greeuance
than these, which now being satisfied doo not much annoie me.
Therefore' saith Malcolme, 'suffer me to remaine where I am,
least if I atteine to the regiment of your realme, mine vnquenchable auarice may prooue such; that ye would thinke
the displeasures which now grieue you, should seeme easie in
respect of the vnmeasurable outrage, which might insue
through my comming amongst you.'

Makduffe to this made answer, how it was a far woorse fault than
the other: 'for auarice is the root of all mischiefe, and for that crime
the most part of our kings haue beene slaine and brought to
their finall end. Yet notwithstanding follow my counsell, and
take vpon thee the crowne. There is gold and riches inough in
Scotland to satisfie thy greedie desire.' Then said Malcolme
againe, 'I am furthermore inclined to dissimulation, telling of
leasings, and all other kinds of deceit, so that I naturallie re-
ioise in nothing so much, as to betraie & deceiue such as put

anie trust or confidence in my woords. Then sith there is nothing that more becommeth a prince than constancie, veritie,
truth, and iustice, with the other laudable fellowship of those
faire and noble vertues which are comprehended onelie in
soothfastnesse, and that lieng vtterlie ouerthroweth the same;
you see how vnable I am to gouerne anie prouince or region:
and therefore sith you haue remedies to cloke and hide all the
rest of my other vices, I praie you find shift to cloke this vice
amongst the residue.'

Then said Makduffe: 'This yet is the woorst of all, and there I
leaue thee, and therefore saie; Oh ye vnhappie and miserable
Scotishmen, which are thus scourged with so manie and sundrie calamities, ech one aboue other! Ye haue one curssed and
wicked tyrant that now reigneth ouer you, without anie right
or title, oppressing you with his most bloudie crueltie. This
other that hath the right to the crowne, is so replet with the
inconstant behauiour and manifest vices of Englishmen, that
he is nothing woorthie to inioy it: for by his owne confession
he is not onelie auaritious, and giuen to vnsatiable lust, but so
false a traitor withall, that no trust is to be had vnto anie
woord he speaketh. Adieu Scotland, for now I account my
selfe a banished man for euer, without comfort or consolation':
and with those woords the brackish tears trickled downe his
cheekes verie abundantlie.

At the last, when he was readie to depart, Malcolme tooke him
by the sleeue, and said: 'Be of good comfort Makduffe, for I
haue none of these vices before remembred, but haue iested
with thee in this manner, onelie to prooue thy mind: for diuerse
times heeretofore hath Makbeth sought by this manner of
meanes to bring me into his hands, but the more slow I haue
shewed my selfe to condescend to thy motion and request, the
more diligence shall I vse in accomplishing the same.' Incon-
tinentlie heerevpon they imbraced ech other, and promising
to be faithfull the one to the other, they fell in consultation
how they might best prouide for all their businesse, to bring
the same to good effect. Soone after, Makduffe repairing to the
borders of Scotland, addressed his letters with secret dispatch

vnto the nobles of the realme, declaring how Malcolme was confederat with him, to come hastilie into Scotland to claime the crowne, and therefore he required them, sith he was right inheritor thereto, to assist him with their powers to recouer the same out of the hands of the wrongfull vsurper.

In the meane time, Malcolme purchased such fauor at king Edwards hands, that old Siward earle of Northumberland was appointed with ten thousand men to go with him into Scotland, to support him in this enterprise, for recouerie of his right. After these newes were spread abroad in Scotland, the nobles drew into two seuerall factions, the one taking part with Makbeth, and the other with Malcolme. Heerevpon insued often-times sundrie bickerings, & diuerse light skirmishes: for those that were of Malcolmes side, would not ieopard to ioine with their enimies in a pight field, till his comming out of England to their support. But after that Makbeth perceiued his enimies power to increase, by such aid as came to them foorth of Eng-land with his aduersarie Malcolme, he recoiled backe into Fife, there purposing to abide in campe fortified, at the castell of Dunsinane, and to fight with his enimies, if they ment to pursue him; howbeit some of his friends aduised him, that it should be best for him, either to make some agreement with Malcolme, or else to flee with all speed into the Iles, and to take his treas-ure with him, to the end he might wage sundrie great princes of the realme to take his part, & reteine strangers, in whome he might better trust than in his owne subiects, which stale dailie from him: but he had such confidence in his prophesies, that he beleeued he should neuer be vanquished, till Birnane wood were brought to Dunsinane; nor yet to be slaine with anie man, that should be or was borne of anie woman.

Malcolme following hastilie after Makbeth, came the night before the battell vnto Birnane wood, and when his armie had rested a while there to refresh them, he commanded euerie man to get a bough of some tree or other of that wood in his hand as big as he might beare, and to march foorth therewith in such wise, that on the next morrow they might come closelie and without sight in this manner within viewe of his enimies. On the morrow when Makbeth beheld them comming in this sort, he first maruelled what the matter ment, but in the end remembred himselfe that the prophesie which he had heard long before that time, of the comming of Birnane wood to Dunsinane castell, was likelie to be now fulfilled. Neuerthelesse, he brought his men in order of battell, and exhorted them to doo valiantlie, howbeit his enimies had scarselie cast from them their boughs, when Makbeth perceiuing their numbers, betooke him streict to flight, whom Makduffe pursued with great hatred euen till he came vnto Lunfannaine, where Makbeth perceiuing that Makduffe was hard at his backe, leapt beside his horsse, saieng; 'Thou traitor, what meaneth it that thou shouldest thus in vaine follow me that am not appointed to be slaine by anie creature that is borne of a woman, come on therefore, and receiue thy reward which thou hast deserued for thy paines,' and therewithall he lifted vp his swoord thinking to haue slaine him.

But Makduffe quicklie auoiding from his horsse, yer he came at him, answered (with his naked swoord in his hand) saieng: 'It is true Makbeth, and now shall thine insatiable crueltie haue an end, for I am euen he that thy wizzards haue told thee of, who was neuer borne of my mother, but ripped out of her wombe': therewithall he stept vnto him, and slue him in the place. Then cutting his head from his shoulders, he set it vpon a pole, and brought it vnto Malcolme. This was the end of Makbeth, after he had reigned 17 yeeres ouer the Scotishmen. In the beginning of his reigne he accomplished manie woorthie acts, verie profitable to the common-wealth (as ye haue heard), but afterward by illusion of the diuell, he defamed the same with most terrible crueltie. He was slaine in the yeere of the incarnation 1057, and in the 16 yeere of king Edwards reigne ouer the Englishmen. (Pp. 174-6.)

Any reader of these excerpts will observe that Shakespeare departs notably from Holinshed in depicting the characters of Macbeth and Lady Macbeth. Holinshed's description of Donwald and his wife does not account for the departure, and it may be that Shakespeare was influenced by other historians of Scotland. Several scholars, Henry Paul most recently, have suggested that he was familiar with the Latin *Rerum Scoticarum Historia* (1582) by George Buchanan, whose portrayal of Macbeth and Lady Macbeth differs considerably from that of Holinshed. The nature of the difference may be seen from the following brief excerpts in Paul's translation:[1]

For Macbeth had keen intelligence, was absolutely high minded and desirous of great things; had moderation been given to him he would have been worthy to exercise power howsoever great.

* * *

By this dream [in Buchanan the meeting with the witches occurs in a dream] his mind, sick with desire and hope, was so profoundly stirred that he kept turning over with himself all the ways for obtaining the kingdom. [Even before the dream he] cherished in his mind a hidden hope of being king.

* * *

His mind, bold enough of itself, was spurred on by the almost daily taunts of his wife, who shared all of his plans.

* * *

The stings of the king's murder drove his overwrought mind to a precipice, as he turned his rule gained by perfidy into a cruel tyranny.

1. See Paul, pp. 213–17; Buchanan, pp. 72–3.

APPENDIX C

Reading List

A. C. Bradley, '*Macbeth,*' *Shakespearean Tragedy*, London, Macmillan, 1904.

C. Brooks, 'The Naked Babe and the Cloak of Manliness,' *The Well Wrought Urn*, New York, Reynal and Hitchcock, 1947.

T. De Quincey, 'On the Knocking at the Gate in *Macbeth*' (1823), *Miscellaneous Essays*, Boston, 1851.

W. Farnham, '*Macbeth,*' *Shakespeare's Tragic Frontier*, Berkeley, University of California Press, 1950.

F. Fergusson, '*Macbeth* as the Imitation of an Action,' *English Institute Essays 1951*, New York, Columbia University Press, 1952.

G. W. Knight, 'Brutus and Macbeth' and '*Macbeth* and the Metaphysic of Evil,' *The Wheel of Fire*, Oxford, Oxford University Press, 1930.

L. C. Knights, "How Many Children Had Lady Macbeth," *Explorations*, New York, Stewart, 1947.

H. N. Paul, *The Royal Play of Macbeth*, New York, Macmillan, 1950.

E. E. Stoll, '*Macbeth,*' *Art and Artifice in Shakespeare*, Cambridge, Cambridge University Press, 1938.

E. M. W. Tillyard, '*Macbeth,*' *Shakespeare's History Plays*, New York, Macmillan, 1946.

R. Walker, *The Time Is Free*, London, Andrew Dakers, 1949.